SHIBBOLETH

# LIT Z

Sara Guyer and Brian McGrath, series editors

Lit Z embraces models of criticism uncontained by conventional notions of history, periodicity, and culture, and committed to the work of reading. Books in the series may seem untimely, anachronistic, or out of touch with contemporary trends because they have arrived too early or too late. Lit Z creates a space for books that exceed and challenge the tendencies of our field and in doing so reflect on the concerns of literary studies here and abroad.

At least since Friedrich Schlegel, thinking that affirms literature's own untimeliness has been named romanticism. Recalling this history, Lit Z exemplifies the survival of romanticism as a mode of contemporary criticism, as well as forms of contemporary criticism that demonstrate the unfulfilled possibilities of romanticism. Whether or not they focus on the romantic period, books in this series epitomize romanticism as a way of thinking that compels another relation to the present. Lit Z is the first book series to take seriously this capacious sense of romanticism.

In 1977, Paul de Man and Geoffrey Hartman, two scholars of romanticism, team-taught a course called Literature Z that aimed to make an intervention into the fundamentals of literary study. Hartman and de Man invited students to read a series of increasingly difficult texts and through attention to language and rhetoric compelled them to encounter "the bewildering variety of ways such texts could be read." The series' conceptual resonances with that class register the importance of recollection, reinvention, and reading to contemporary criticism. Its books explore the creative potential of reading's untimeliness and history's enigmatic force.

# Shibboleth

JUDGES, DERRIDA, CELAN

*Marc Redfield*

FORDHAM UNIVERSITY PRESS   NEW YORK 2021

Copyright © 2021 Fordham University Press

All rights reserved. No part of this publication may be reproduced, stored in a retrieval system, or transmitted in any form or by any means—electronic, mechanical, photocopy, recording, or any other—except for brief quotations in printed reviews, without the prior permission of the publisher.

Fordham University Press has no responsibility for the persistence or accuracy of URLs for external or third-party Internet websites referred to in this publication and does not guarantee that any content on such websites is, or will remain, accurate or appropriate.

Fordham University Press also publishes its books in a variety of electronic formats. Some content that appears in print may not be available in electronic books.

Visit us online at www.fordhampress.com.

Library of Congress Cataloging-in-Publication Data available online at https://catalog.loc.gov.

Printed in the United States of America

23  22  21    5  4  3  2  1

First edition

## Contents

1 Shibboleth: Inheritance   1
2 שיבולת: Judges   13
3 S(h)ibboleth: Sovereign Violence and the Remainder   19
4 *Schibboleth*: Derrida   36
5 Schibboleth: Celan   50
6 "S(ch)ibboleth": Apostrophe   69
7 S(c)hibboleth: Babel   86
8 *Shibboleth*: Salcedo   100

ACKNOWLEDGMENTS   107

NOTES   109

INDEX   155

# SHIBBOLETH

# 1
# Shibboleth
*Inheritance*

Although this study is not quite about a word, it circles around something like a word: *shibboleth*—a bit of language that turns spectral as we linger over it, as Walter Benjamin's much-cited citation might lead us to expect: "Words too can have their aura. Karl Kraus has described it thus: 'The closer you look at a word, the more distantly it looks back.'"[1] Any word, on the authority of that epigram, has the potential to make palpable its participation in the withdrawal of language. But *shibboleth* poses singular complications. As a closer look will show, it is less, more, and other than a word; and to the extent that it is one, no language can properly claim it. It owes these complications to a narrative that made it unusually mobile, capable of traveling from one end to the other of recorded history, and across any number of languages. For *shibboleth* is of course a loanword from Judeo-Christian deep time. As a feminine noun it appears five times in the Hebrew Bible:[2] three times to mean something like flowing stream or flood (Psalm 69:2; Psalm 69:15; Isaiah 27:12); once to mean ears of grain (Job 24:24); once, in the passage in Judges 12 that made it famous and that we shall be examining, possibly to mean stream, possibly ears of grain, but most immediately, in the context of the text, nothing at all, since there it is used solely as a pronunciation test by the Gileadites in order to identify their defeated enemy, the Ephraimites:

> And the Gileadites took the passages of Jordan before the Ephraimites: and it was so, that when those Ephraimites which were escaped said, Let me go over; that the men of Gilead said unto him, Art thou an Ephraimite? If he said, Nay; then said they unto him, Say now Shibboleth: and he said Sibboleth: for he could not frame to pronounce it right. Then they took him, and slew him at the passages of Jordan: and there fell at that time of the Ephraimites forty and two thousand.[3]

In times, cultures, and languages far removed from those of ancient Israel, the word *shibboleth* came to signify the sort of test it was supposedly once used to set: a test in which a hard-to-falsify sign winnows identities and establishes and confirms borders. Ancillary meanings developed to a greater or lesser extent in different languages. French usage hews relatively closely to the biblical story: Hachette defines *shibboleth* as *"test, épreuve décisive"*; the Grand Robert has *"épreuve décisive qui fait juger de la capacité d'une personne"* (a decisive test that tries a person's abilities). German usage is broader, as the succinct Duden entry for *Schibboleth* indicates: *"Erkennungszeichen; Losungswort; Merkmal"* (identifying mark; password, watchword, slogan; distinguishing mark).[4] English is unique in having developed meanings for *shibboleth* that have overtaken and displaced the biblically oriented sense of test-word or identifying trait. Extending further the German extension of the word toward "slogan," modern English grants to *shibboleth* a range of meanings distributed between the poles of test-word and formulaic speech. The entry for *shibboleth* in the online resource Dictionary.com runs thus: "1. a peculiarity of pronunciation, behavior, mode of dress, etc., that distinguishes a particular class or set of persons; 2. a slogan; catchword; 3. a common saying or belief with little current meaning or truth." By the mid–twentieth century that third definition had become dominant—a fact that inspired the opinionated 1965 edition of *Fowler's Modern English Usage* to proclaim that "*shibboleth* is a WORSENED WORD. Ability to pronounce it properly was the means by which Jephthah distinguished his own Gileadites from the refugee Ephraimites among them. . . . It is now rarely used except in the sense of a catchword adopted by a party or sect, especially one that is old-fashioned and repeated as a parrot-cry, appealing to emotion rather than reason. . . . Sometimes it seems to be thought of merely as an ornamental synonym of maxim or cliché."[5] Current English-language dictionaries tend to bear this out, as the online Oxford English Dictionary's one-sentence entry underscores as it unfolds: "A custom, principle, or belief distinguishing a particular class or group of people, especially a long-standing one regarded as outmoded or no longer important."[6] The English-language Wikipedia entry opens with a similar statement: "A shibboleth is either a saying that people repeatedly cite that some think to be wrong, or a word or custom whose variations in pronunciation or style distinguish members of ingroups from those of outgroups, with an implicit value judgment based on knowledge of the shibboleth."[7]

Without pretending to be able to account historico-philologically for the vicissitudes of this word in post–seventeenth century English, we can sketch a rationale for a semantic cluster roughly mappable as: test-word; password;

identifying mark; slogan; cliché.⁸ For the multiple meanings of *shibboleth* in English seem intriguingly keyed to certain large aspects of modern life, insofar as these meanings tend to refer back to their own technical reproducibility, while taking up different positions on an axis of publicity and privacy on the one hand and of semantic and nonsemantic functioning on the other. Passwords presuppose secrecy whereas clichés, slogans, and test-words presuppose various degrees of knownness (the cliché circulates as the already known; the slogan imposes itself; the test-word presents itself as a challenge that involves what one might call a certain open secrecy). Passwords and test-words bracket their own semantic functioning, though along different vectors: passwords, particularly in the machine age, rapidly leave the domain of the logos and cease to be pronounceable words; test-words at least in principle remain pronounceable, but, unlike passwords, they insist on a performance irreducible to knowledge or will (this forms the nucleus of the problematic that will detain us when we examine *shibboleth* as test-word in the biblical sense). Clichés and slogans retain a semantic dimension—slogans more fully, if they are to remain effective perlocutionary performances, whereas clichés, to the extent that they have lost "current meaning or truth," approach the state of contentless, mass-mechanical iteration suggested by the origins of the word *cliché* itself in nineteenth-century print technology.⁹ All of these avatars of the English word *shibboleth*, however, the password as well as the cliché, directly or indirectly remark their dependence on their own iterability and indeed on a potentially uncontrollable iterability. All of them also put pressure on the semantic functioning of language—even the slogan, however heartfelt its repetition might be in a particular context, cannot avoid hinting at its own potential collapse into emptily mechanical reiteration. The semantic field that English calls *shibboleth* references the waning of the logos in an era of technical reproducibility. This word also seems to cue more punctually historical phenomena: the proliferation of tests, passwords, and checkpoints in digitalized, stratified, fragmented, and heavily (if, in wealthy zones, discreetly) policed societies that direct substantial resources to the filtering of populations; the hyperproduction and instantaneous outdatedness of signs, texts, and images under technically advanced consumer capitalism, with a concomitant emptying out of political institutions and an ever-increasing subordination of social life to the logic of the cash nexus and its language of equivalence; a refugee crisis of global scale that grows more acute with each passing year, as resources and civic viability continue to be stripped from the "outer zone," to use a term offered by Alphonso Lingis some two decades ago, with wealth concentrated ever more densely in an international "archipelago of technopoles."[10]

One could heap up other such shibboleths to describe the era of the shibboleth. The mood of such reflections tends toward the dystopic, with all the darkly sublime excitations of that genre; though of course many of the phenomena under consideration form part of the banality of the everyday. "In the era of cyber-surveillance," as Emily Apter comments, "checkpoints can be as anodyne as a Facebook wall, a paywall, or a document fingerprint, or as menacing as a citizen's authorization to apply a stand-your-ground law."[11] At present millions of digital passwords (including one dedicated to verifying, in certain contexts, the identity of the present writer) are managed by "Shibboleth," an "open-source software project" that claims to be "among the world's most widely deployed federated identity solutions, connecting users to applications both within and between organizations."[12] The name was well chosen, and it can serve as a metonym for innumerable contemporary technologies and practices that go far beyond mere password management: shibboleth technologies, as we may call them, of encryption and decryption, exclusion and inclusion, identification, privatization, exposure. Neoliberal ideologies, along with the economic, political, military, technological, and cultural phenomena we sum up as globalization, are unimaginable in the absence of such technologies, which flourish particularly when zones of indeterminacy are being created and leveraged. The binary logic of testing has a natural affinity with contexts in which it has become necessary or expedient to generate, parse, and police identities.[13] But here again we seem to be touching on a particular determination of a much broader phenomenon: a testing imperative, ancient as metaphysics but particularly coercive in the modern era, infiltrating seemingly every aspect of life in a context in which the drawing and blurring of borders saturates cultural, political, semiotic, and economic space.[14] Testing mechanisms can be subtle or crude, technically sophisticated or phantasmatic and wild. The ethnic nationalism and transnational racism that, throughout the modern era, accompany the deracinating movement of global capital, are reaction formations laced with the same drives and anxieties as the techno-capitalist regime against which they react; which is why all modern racisms, no matter how fiercely invested in fantasies of intuitive certainty, hunger for supplemental fixes and highs, from the high-tech allure of genetic testing to the atavistic-sadistic jolt of stereotype and myth.

These large-format considerations suggest that there is something to be gained from focusing on the traditional, and, in non-English-language contexts, still current, meaning of *shibboleth* as test-word. It will be useful, furthermore, to center attention on the "word" *shibboleth* "itself" (we shall see very soon how loose-fingered a grip the word "word" has on this word). The analysis thereby acquires far more manageable contours, since, despite its transhistorical and translinguistic survival skills and its vast reserves of exemplarity, the word *shibboleth* appears rarely in the Western literary and philosophical archive. In English, *shibboleth* rhymes fortuitously with *death*, and one might have expected that rhyme to show up occasionally in standard poetry anthologies, but a couplet in Milton's *Samson Agonistes* offers almost the only occasion on which readers of canonical British poetry encounter it. Early on in that text, the Chorus, seeking to console the enslaved, blind, and bitter Samson, reminds him of Israel's frequent ingratitude toward great leaders, offering examples from stories in Judges that precede his:

> Thy words to my remembrance bring
> How *Succoth* and the Fort of *Penuel*
> Thir great Deliverer contemn'd,
> The matchless *Gideon* in pursuit
> Of Madian and her vanquish'd Kings:
> And how ingrateful *Ephraim*
> Had dealt with *Jephtha*, who by argument,
> Not worse than by his shield and spear
> Defended *Israel* from the *Ammonite*,
> Had not his prowess quell'd thir pride
> In that sore battel when so many dy'd
> Without Reprieve adjudg'd to death,
> For want of well pronouncing *Shibboleth*.[15]

Alert readers may well hear more in these lines than the Chorus at least seems to intend, since the episodes being recalled showcase not just the fickleness of relatives but also the alacrity with which leaders direct lethal violence against fickle relatives (Gideon slaughters the men of Succoth and Penuel on his way back from killing the Midian princes in Judges 8; Jephthah, leader of the Gileadites, slaughters the Ephraimites after defeating Ammon in Judges 12). It is possible to glimpse a killing field being adumbrated in these lines—a space ready to host Samson's mass-murderous suicide. But however one interprets this speech, it hardly ranks among the most important in Milton's tragedy, and the word *shibboleth*, despite its emphatic positioning, carries little more than metrical stress. It seems generally to be the case that this word, on its rare appearances in the literary record, garners less emphasis than a scholar setting out to write a study of it might have expected.[16] An exception will be found in a scene in William Faulkner's *Absalom, Absalom!* (1936) in which Rosa Coldfield tells of running toward her niece Judith Sutpen (whose fiancé Charles Bon has just been shot by Judith's brother Henry) and being halted—ambiguously and momentarily, yet also devastatingly—by a touch of the hand of Clytemnestra Sutpen, Judith's black half-sister. In this section of the novel, Rosa's narrative is given to us in italics, one of the many ways in which the novel marks the writtenness of its fictions of oral transmission:

> *Then she touched me and then did I stop dead. Possibly even then my body did not stop. . . . I know only that my entire being seemed to run at blind full tilt into something monstrous and immobile, with a shocking impact too soon and too quick to be mere amazement and outrage at that black arresting and untimorous hand on my white woman's flesh. . . . But let flesh touch with flesh, and watch the fall of all the eggshell shibboleth of caste and color too.*[17]

Even pulled from context, this passage has enough figurative density to arrest and touch a reader. As a passage about passage, it projects the biblical story of a perilous border-crossing onto the broad modern meaning of *shibboleth* as identifying mark, while troubling the identity of that identifying mark through an adjective, "eggshell," that always already, even before its "fall," connotes fragility and fragmentation (it being an eggshell's purpose to shatter) and hints at the destruction of the legibility of the text's binary racial code (eggshells being, in the absence of further specification, possibly white, possibly not). In context, this textual knot grows yet more complex, for the novel's plot has as its vanishing point the (elaborately unreliable) story of Thomas Sutpen performing an ur-act of crossing over, fashioning himself into a white planter-class patriarch after being refused entry, as a ragged messenger boy, by a black slave to the front door of a grand house. Rosa repeats that motif here as a fragmented act of (non)passage (she "stops dead" but her body "possibly" does not, a paradox that this hallucinogenic scene elaborates and complicates over several pages);[18] and that aporetic movement replays in miniature the double bind of the Sutpen story, which compulsively reproduces the possible illegibility of the racial identities that it exists to produce and secure. We shall return to *Absalom, Absalom!* and clarify these points a little later. For now it suffices to note the complexity with which the word *shibboleth* punctuates the novel's central motif of passing and passing over (and failing to pass over). Not until Paul Celan will *shibboleth* achieve richer literary elaboration.

Appearances of this word in the philosophical record are infrequent. Thanks to the magic of searchable databases it is possible to state without bravado that the word *Schibboleth* does not appear anywhere in Kant or Fichte or Nietzsche or (perhaps surprisingly) Benjamin.[19] Hegel uses it three times, Marx five or six, and Adorno twice, mostly in polemical contexts that nudge the German *Schibboleth* in the direction of the well-established English meaning of cliché.[20] (This is particularly true of Marx, the great satirist of bourgeois commonplaces: e.g., "By all means, production, production on a constantly increasing scale, runs the shibboleth").[21] The word appears three times in Freud's later writing, at points where Freud is affirming the boundaries constituting the institutional and doctrinal integrity of psychoanalysis. Thus in a footnote added in 1920 to *Three Essays on the Theory of Sexuality* (1905), Freud asserts that the recognition of "the importance of the Oedipus complex . . . has become the shibboleth that distinguishes the adherents of psycho-analysis from its opponents"; in *The Ego and the Id* (1923), he affirms that "the division of the psychical into what is conscious and unconscious" constitutes "the first shibboleth of psycho-analysis"; and in the *New Introductory Lectures* (1932), he tells us that the "strangeness of the assertions" of the psycho-analytic theory of dreams "has made [that theory] play the part of a shibboleth, the use of which decided who could become a follower of psycho-analysis and to whom it remained forever incomprehensible."[22] In these passages, *Schibboleth* has its classic meaning of test-word or recognition-sign, *Erkennungszeichen*, a sign that polices a border. It gathers up and incorporates Freud's fierce desire to claim psychoanalysis as his progeny and legacy, and to control the development of psychoanalysis both as a theory and as an institution. That the first two of these *Schibboleths* evoke dramas of recognition (Oedipus) and division (between conscious and unconscious systems) lends extra resonance to the third; for the "strangeness," the *Fremdartigkeit*, of the dream-theory, and by extension psychoanalysis generally, consists in its being a theory of *mis*recognition and division-violation—a theory of ambivalence, spectrality, illicit border-crossing. From that angle we could say that, in erecting psychoanalysis into a password to and for itself, Freud at once represses and calls forth a ghostly double for that shibboleth—one that cannot but misspeak itself, out of turn, with an uncertain accent, from an other place. (As Freud comments, "the unconscious speaks many dialects": it exists to crack and generate codes and to send emissaries over the line.) Any study of *shibboleth* will need to draw inspiration from psychoanalysis, a discourse propelled like no other by shibboleth-effects—not, or not just, in an abstract or thematic sense, but quite concretely or materially as an insistent foregrounding of words that grant, forbid, delay or simulate access to other scenes, voices, and signifiers: words misspoken, forgotten and returning, errant, promiscuous, at work in the *arrière-scene*, punning across languages, having letters purloined, coming unglued.[23]

*Schibboleth* is a rare word in Paul Celan's oeuvre, as it is elsewhere in the archive; but the two poems of Celan's that showcase it do so with such power that Jacques Derrida was led to grant exemplary status to this word in his influential *Schibboleth: Pour Paul Celan* (1986). These texts by Celan and Derrida thus form something of a salient. They offer us the chance to reflect on poetic and philosophical readings of a figure that seems at once marginal and central in the Western tradition—visible only as a hairline crack, though perhaps one as consequent, in its own way, as the "barely perceptible fissure" marking Poe's House of Usher ("which, extending from the roof of the building in front, made its way down the wall in a zigzag direction, until it became lost in the sullen waters of the tarn").[24] When we bracket the large issues evoked earlier in order to focus on *shibboleth* as word and concept as bequeathed by the biblical narrative, we simplify matters in one way only to complicate them in another, for we find ourselves parsing fundamental questions of identity and difference that play themselves out in a context of extreme violence. The force of a test-word resides in its resistance to knowledge or willpower, as noted earlier, and this force is nothing if not lethal.[25] In the story in Judges, "forty-two thousand" Ephraimites fail the shibboleth-test and are killed at the border; the number, though almost certainly symbolic, suggests mass murder on a nearly genocidal scale. As has already been hinted, however, the possibility of this deadly sorting-system derives from a more general condition of iterability that renders all borders and all codes permeable, and all technologies of targeting vulnerable to error, as Derrida's classic analyses have demonstrated in numerous contexts.[26] Rather than being a contingent byproduct of the targeting process, finitude inhabits the shibboleth-test from the inside, as it were, opening it to an alterity that is also—and this is one of the major levers, and challenges, of Derrida's thought—constitutive of the singularity of a judgment or event, including the event of a poem. Somewhat paradoxically, given its blood-soaked origins, the figure of the shibboleth thus becomes, in Celan and Derrida, the watchword of an affirmative, antifascist politics.[27] Or better, it *also* becomes this; Derrida will stress "the terrifying ambiguity of the *shibboleth*, sign of belonging and threat of discrimination, indiscernible discernment between alliance and war" (48).[28] The following pages develop that claim by examining the concept and performance of the shibboleth in texts that Derrida's wide-ranging reading of Celan privileges but does not examine in detail: the biblical story and the poems that Celan titled "In eins" and "Schibboleth." In closing we shall look briefly at Doris Salcedo's famous installation at the Tate Modern, *Shibboleth* (2007), the title of which—probably with intentional reference to Derrida and Celan—offers another affirmation of the critical and aesthetic resources discoverable in this thin, raveled strand of linguistic inheritance.

# 2
# שיבולת
*Judges*

The mixture of legend and chronicle making up the Book of Judges describes a fragmented Israel trapped in a cycle of backsliding from God, enslavement by foreign powers, redemption, and reempowerment followed by renewed backsliding: a world in which each tribe follows its own interests and directs bellicose energy as readily against another tribe of Israel as against Israel's traditional enemies. The phrase, repeated four times in the later chapters of Judges, "In those days there was no king in Israel: every man did that which was right in his own eyes," forms the closing sentence of the book, where it glosses the gruesome story of the Levite whose concubine is raped to death by members of the tribe of Benjamin, and who cuts her body ("together with her bones") into twelve parts to form messages to the other tribes; those tribes then nearly annihilate Benjamin in the Battle of Gibeah, sparing only a few men so that the tribe will survive. (Since the Benjamite women have all been murdered, the remaining men are married off to women from a town, Jabesh-Gilead, that had refused to join in the war against the

Benjamites, and that, both as punishment and as a way of generating a supply of wives, has had all its men slaughtered [Judges 19–21]).[1] Given that the tribes of Israel not only kill "twenty and five thousand" Benjamite warriors in battle, but then go on to massacre the entire Benjamite population (20:46–48), this all-but-genocidal episode holds up as the worst *bellum internecinum* in Judges. Running it a close second, however—and far outstripping it in adult male casualties, the casualties that the Bible counts—is the battle between the Gileadites and the Ephraimites earlier in Judges that culminates in the shibboleth test with its "forty and two thousand" Ephraimite victims.

The story of the shibboleth test forms the capstone to the story of Jephthah in Judges 11–12, which begins with a small-scale version of social fragmentation: "Now Jephthah the Gileadite was a mighty man of valor, and he was the son of an harlot: and Gilead begat Jephthah. And Gilead's wife bare him sons; and his wife's sons grew up, and they thrust out Jephthah, and said unto him, Thou shalt not inherit in our father's house; for thou are the son of a strange woman" (11:1–2). ("Gilead," very occasionally a proper name in the Bible, but commonly a toponym for an area of the Transjordan, is perhaps functioning here as a collective personification, with no specified genealogy leading to Jephthah.) When the Ammonites oppress Israel, however, the elders of Gilead seek him out and ask him to lead them in battle. The first sign that speech acts will play an important role in the narrative comes as Jephthah bargains for sovereignty: he will lead the Gileadites against the Ammonites if they in turn will not just reintegrate him, but make him their permanent leader (*shofet* or "judge"), which they swear to do: "The Lord be witness between us, if we do not do so according to thy words." Jephthah in turn makes a vow: "And Jephthah vowed a vow unto the Lord, and said, if thou shalt without fail de-

שיבולת: JUDGES

liver the children of Ammon into mine hands, then it shall be, that whatsoever cometh forth of the doors of my house to meet me, when I return in peace from the children of Ammon, shall surely be the Lord's, and I will offer it up for a burnt offering" (11:30–31). As mythic narrative demands, what comes forth out of the doors of his house, after the battle, is his own, and only, child. The child, a daughter who remains unnamed in the story—there is a sense in which she does not live long enough for a name—begs for two months to "bewail her virginity," which are accorded her, after which the father "did with her according to his vow which he had vowed: and she knew no man" (11:38).[2]

In the wake of this blood sacrifice—the only narratively foregrounded case of consummated child sacrifice in the Bible[3]—the Ephraimites cross the Jordan and enter Gilead, angry that Jephthah has fought (and presumably despoiled) the Ammonites without them. There follows the famous story of the shibboleth test:

> And the men of Ephraim gathered themselves together, and went northward, and said unto Jephthah, Wherefore passedst thou over to fight against the children of Ammon, and didst not call us to go with thee? we will burn thine house upon thee with fire. And Jephthah said unto them, I and my people were at great strife with the children of Ammon; and when I called you, ye delivered me not out of their hands. And when I saw that ye delivered me not, I put my life in my hands, and passed over against the children of Ammon, and the LORD delivered them into my hand: wherefore then are ye come up unto me this day, to fight against me? Then Jephthah gathered together all the men of Gilead, and fought with Ephraim: and the men of Gilead smote

Ephraim, because they said, Ye Gileadites are
fugitives of Ephraim among the Ephraimites, and
among the Manassites. And the Gileadites took the
passages of Jordan before the Ephraimites: and it
was so, that when those Ephraimites which were
escaped said, Let me go over; that the men of
Gilead said unto him, Art thou an Ephraimite? If he
said, Nay; then said they unto him, Say now Shibboleth [שיבולת]: and he said Sibboleth [סיבולת]: for he
could not frame to pronounce it right. Then they
took him, and slew him at the passages of Jordan: and
there fell at that time of the Ephraimites forty and
two thousand. (12:1–6)

In passing we may note that the Hebrew text displays peculiarities in the passage in which the Ephraimites undergo
their linguistic test. The phonetic difference on which the
story turns most likely had to be misrepresented in order to
receive written representation. It is not clear how the historical Gileadites would have pronounced the word *shibboleth*,
nor how the Ephraimites would have mispronounced it; the
decisive sound may well have been an English-style *th*, a bit
of Proto-Semitic retained in the Gileadic dialect to which no
letter corresponded in ancient Hebraic script, leading to the
word's being written with an initial *shin* consonant in Judges.
Ironically, the Ephraimitic pronunciation was possibly some
kind of *sh*—though also possibly some kind of *s*, or *t*, or *th*.[4]
In all of these cases, since the letter *shin* was being used to
represent the sound the Gileadites were requesting, and since
in unpointed Hebrew script, *shin* and *sin* are indistinguish-
able, the text had to use a different s-letter, the *samekh*, to
render the Ephraimitic articulation of the word. "To advance
the point of the anecdote," as Jack M. Sasson puts it, "a word
was purposely (or not) misspelled by using the consonant

*samekh* (ס), instead of the expected *shin* (שׁ). The scribe might have had another option, which was to use the *sin* (שׂ), but avoided it, at least because it was orthographically undistinguishable from *shin* and might have compromised the thrust of the story."[5] A misspelling, or better, a graphic trope, is required in order to produce a stable, writable, and readable difference that relays the all-important phonemic difference (whatever it was). The text itself, as a written performance, mimics the Ephraimite's misspeaking through an act of miswriting and could thus be said—a little fancifully, but in the spirit of honoring the hyperbolic force of these microscopic differences—to violate or fail the shibboleth test even as it generates it. This contingency serves as our first index of a structural, noncontingent fallibility that forms the condition of possibility of shibboleth tests.

Before pursuing that large question, however, we may follow to its end the story of Jephthah—which will not take long, since it concludes with an abrupt final verse after the shibboleth story. "And Jephthah judged Israel six years. Then died Jephthah the Gileadite, and was buried in one of the cities of Gilead" (12:7). The words "one of" were added by the King James Version translators, and many editions italicize them so as to flag the insertion. Jephthah's is the shortest reign of all the judges; he dies without progeny; and Sasson notes that "he is said to be buried not in Mizpah or even Tov, but 'in the towns of Gilead,' lacking the precise location normally attached to judges. Expanding on this odd phrasing, the rabbis had Jephthah die in battle, with portions of his body scattered all around—a small price to pay for his bad judgment."[6] (A marginal note to an Aramaic commentary adds extra graphic detail: "And his limbs fell from him and his limbs were buried in the cities of Gilead.")[7] By "bad judgment" Sasson has in mind not just Jephthah's sacrifice of his daughter, but also his murderous response to the

Ephraimites. Earlier in Judges the Ephraimites had been summoned by the Benjamite leader Ehud and had held the fords of the Jordan with him against Moab (3:27–29); summoned by the Manassite leader Gideon, they had held the fords alone against Midian (7:24–8:3). Although these various stories in Judges are not chronologically marked, by the time we get to Jephthah, narrative sequence has established the Ephraimites as reliable partners in a judge's battles with Israel's enemies (though in the Gideon story we also get some foreshadowing: the Ephraimites complain to Gideon about having been called late into battle; he soothes them with diplomatic words, and then, as we noted earlier, goes on to murder the male population of Succoth and Penuel, cities that had refused his call to arms [8:1–3]). Furthermore, the dominant narrative strands of the Pentateuch suggest that the Ephraimites are right to claim close kinship with the Gileadites.[8] But kinship here works as a taunt: "and the men of Gilead smote Ephraim, because they said, Ye Gileadites are fugitives of Ephraim among the Ephraimites, and among the Manassites." The story of Jephthah contributes substantially to the social fragmentation that looms large at this point in the Bible. Of questionable legitimacy, destructive of his own progeny, ferociously murderous toward a closely related tribe, a judge of short reign whose nonspecific place of burial hints at a scattered corpse, Jephthah seems to be acting out an autoimmune disorder within patriarchal culture. His disastrous vow, which links his sovereignty and his prowess in war to the extinction of his line, may have something to do with the blend of massive force and structural instability that characterizes the shibboleth test as a technology of border control.

## Chapter 3
# S(h)ibboleth
*Sovereign Violence and the Remainder*

The story of the shibboleth test has had paradigmatic power. In the wake of this narrative, the word *shibboleth*, in all its manifold spellings and pronunciations at different times and in different languages, has become the concept of the test that the narrative describes. In becoming a common noun that means the use to which it is put in the story, *shibboleth* extends itself immeasurably past its immediate context; but it is helpful to begin with a consideration of the paradigm—a pronunciation test that presupposes both a telling linguistic difference and a great deal of linguistic and cultural similarity between two warring groups, one of which, having prevailed, holds the power of life and death over the other. Western history records a few cases of mass-murderous shibboleth-testing in this precise sense—the most famous ones all, as it happens, involving French-speaking victims: the "Sicilian Vespers" of March 30, 1282, when Sicilians rebelled against the forces of Charles I, identifying victims— such, at least, is the legend—by having them pronounce the word *ciciru* (chickpea); the "Matins of Bruges" of May 18,

1302, when Flemish fighters slaughtered a garrison installed by Philip IV, using as shibboleth the phrase *schild en vriend* (shield and friend); closer to our time, and more terrible in scale, the "Parsley Massacre" that claimed the lives of thousands of Haitians and Dominicans of Haitian descent, ordered by Rafael Trujillo and carried out on the northwest border of the Dominican Republic in the first week of October 1937 by squadrons that employed as one of their identity tests the Spanish word for parsley, *perejil*.[1]

Such close historical analogues to the biblical story are infrequent, however, and are not our main object of interest here. At issue is the exemplary yet also unruly force of a narrative. Behind the story of the shibboleth test looms the story of Babel, which tells how the Lord "confounded the language of all the earth" and "scattered" humanity "upon the face of all the earth" (Genesis 11:9). We shall eventually want to look again at that extraordinary moment in Genesis; but for now it suffices to note that among the uncountable consequences of Yahweh's confounding and scattering of language is the confounding of confounding itself, such that the differences among languages and peoples can always turn uncertain and contestable, as is the case with the Gileadites and the Ephraimites. "Ye Gileadites are fugitives of Ephraim among the Ephraimites"—the shibboleth test is necessary because the difference between self and other, friend and enemy, family member and stranger, has threatened to become illegible. When the Ephraimite requests, "Let me go over," and then, trying to save his life, answers "No" to the question of whether he is an Ephraimite, he has not yet betrayed himself. The shibboleth test provides a supplement to ordinary discourse in order to establish a difference between a self and an other—a potential infiltrator or, in the biblical story, a potential escapee—who is in some sense a neighbor, looks and sounds like a native, speaks *almost* as "we" do, knows and can perform with native competence *almost* all the codes circulating in the community that is being protected and purged. The other is *almost* the self—and vice versa: the self needs to know its other well in order to select a sign that the other will find hard to feign. Judgments that appear natural and impulsive in contexts in which the other can be imagined as distinct from the self (e.g., the perceived racially, sexually, or culturally marked other; the barbarian whose speech is babble) require the help of a supplemental testing device when a situation turns uncertain. The paradigmatic shibboleth-test, therefore, has an affinity with civil war.

This fraught proximity between self and other renders palpable the performative force of the shibboleth test. It is not just that the test is composed of performatives as speech act theory understands them—a command that includes a modeling of the successful passing of the test that is being demanded ("Say now 'Shibboleth'"), followed by an enforced repetition of the required word that either passes the test or fails it. Speech act theory can only partly account for the force of a test that is also producing the difference for which it asks. The other who might be the self is produced *as* other or self in and through the test that is failed or passed. The pronunciation of the word *shibboleth* is the only guarantee—to the extent that there is a guarantee—that the other is other. Only through the shibboleth test is a nongeographic "internal border" of linguistic difference, as Fichte famously calls it, laid over the "natural" border of the formidable but fordable River Jordan; and only thus, in the punctual unfolding of his enunciation, is the speaker produced as Ephraimite or Gileadite.[2] Two consequences deserve immediate note. In the first place, as Fichte's expression suggests, the linguistic test renders the border mobile, irreducible to fixed sociopolitical articulations of the earth. The biblical story culminates at the Jordan (a logical corralling point, since the Ephraimites are trying to flee to home territory), but in principle the Gileadites could put Ephraimites to the test anywhere they managed to establish a zone of power. The border is now also the checkpoint.[3] Second, and even more significantly, in producing an identity within a field construed as a binary opposition (and it must be stressed here that these identities are *produced*: if we imagine someone who was neither Gileadite nor Ephraimite getting caught up by accident in the dragnet, we would have to add that that person, if judged worthy of being subjected to the shibboleth test, would in principle be processed as either Ephraimite or Gileadite)—in producing these identities, the shibboleth test opens the concept of the political in Carl Schmitt's sense, as the opposition between enemy and friend.[4] Enemy and friend are known only in and through this decisive performance. The greater the uncertainty between these categories, the greater the need for a formalized test in order to produce the border that produces other and self as enemy and friend. On the one hand, the test presupposes for its full formal elaboration a moment of physical domination in which one side holds the power of life or death over the other and can force the other to submit to a test that will decide whether the other lives or dies. The judging instance functions as a finite echo of the divine sovereign claim ("See now that I, even I, am he, and there is no god with me; I kill and I make alive; I wound, and I heal: neither is there any that can deliver out of my hand" [Deuteronomy 32:39]). It compels a speech act into existence and judges it (and in such a context, silence or delaying tactics can always be assimilated to the test and judged accordingly— the test-taker who fails to speak, fails); in this sense the test constitutes an exemplary instance of sovereign power. Yet on the other hand, that sovereign moment depends on the test in order to come into being as such. The shibboleth test provides the only way in which power can obtain a target and realize itself as sovereign, in and through the act of deciding whether to kill or let live.

The performative force of the shibboleth test entails the evacuation of the semantic dimension of the test-word and remains indifferent to cognitive capture from any perspective, including those offered by disciplines such as phonology or phonetics as fields of knowledge. The problem is not just the pragmatic difficulty of cognitively mapping what Ferdinand de Saussure called *actes de parole* ("the pronunciation of even the smallest word represents an infinite number of muscular movements extremely difficult to know and figure").[5] Such knowledge, even if achieved, counts for nothing in the absence of a performance, judged felicitous, of the particular speech act. If it were simply a matter of knowing the meaning or the scientifically formalized elements of a test-word, the test would dissolve into the universality, the open access, of a concept. The Ephraimites presumably *knew* how they ought to be pronouncing a word that had just been pronounced for them (or not: it is possible that they were being tested with a phonic difference they could not hear); be that as it may, they *could not* pronounce it. "It is in the body," Derrida comments, "by reason of a certain impotence coming over their vocal organs, but an impotence of the body proper, of the already cultivated body, limited by a barrier neither organic nor natural, that the Ephraimites experienced their inaptitude to pronounce what they nonetheless knew ought to be pronounced *shibboleth*—and not *sibboleth*."[6] The shibboleth opens the friend/enemy difference as a biopolitical inscription. Like other strong allegories of the articulation of a subject within a field of power— Lacan's name-of-the-father, or the "hey, you" of Althusser's policeman—the story in Judges presents the inscription of the embodied subject in language as an exposure of that subject to political violence in and through noncognitive, performative aspects of language. Such models break with the fiction of a social contract that at some mythical or hypothetical moment in time offered subjectification as a knowable choice. The cut of the shibboleth obtains its material, biopolitical force by bypassing semantics, communication, and cognition; it offers contemporary criticism a further reminder of the necessity yet also the complexity of thinking "the subject" and "the body" as discursively articulated.[7] As the sign of what Derrida calls the "already cultivated body" and thus of a limit that is "neither organic nor natural," the shibboleth opens biopolitics as the phantasmatics of the "native speaker" of a "mother tongue": a tongue that inhabits, shapes, forks, and splits the tongue.

Although the nonsemantic and performative character of the shibboleth as test-word demands analysis along such lines—lines that will need to be extended further—a paradox has also begun to impose itself: the nonsemantic shibboleth test is a site of semantic, conceptual, and theoretical energy. *Shibboleth* becomes "the" shibboleth, the concept of itself. Having lost its semantic and referential dimensions in becoming a test-word (though as soon as we say that it "loses" these dimensions we start losing our way, because as soon as the common-noun-turned-test-word *shibboleth* becomes the concept of itself, it reveals that a nonsense word or a nonsemantic phatic sound or filler or name or expletive would have done just as well for a "shibboleth," so long as the phonemic constraints were being fulfilled)—having become, as test-word, something like a referentless proper name (and indeed, as we shall see, the unspeakable name of God haunts the edges of this story), *shibboleth* folds back onto itself to mean, through a kind of improper antonomasia, an anantonomasia, its own role in the biblical narrative. Indeed, since this role is that of (dis)enabling a perilous crossing, this movement of sublation can be said to translate the movement of translation (*trans-latio, über-setzen*), and to allegorize the sublation of metaphor (*meta-pherein*: a crossing- or bearing-over) into concept that Derrida tracks in his great early essay "White Mythology."[8] "Shibboleth" inflates to signify any linguistic identity test or mark of identity. One can thus claim that as soon as speech begins, the shibboleth leaves its mark, as in Jean-Jacques Rousseau's opening sentence in his *Essay on the Origin of Languages*: "Speech distinguishes man among the animals; language distinguishes the nations among themselves: one does not know where a man comes from until he has spoken."[9] For indeed, any word and any part of a word, spoken aloud, will have greater or lesser shibboleth-test force in the right context (including, to be sure, the word *shibboleth*—in an English-speaking context, for instance, the final "th" offers a trap to speakers of numerous other languages). *Shibboleth* is now no longer a formalized test; it will involve the shading of an accent or turn of phrase, or by extension, nonverbal cues that carry semiotic freight; it gathers to itself all sensory registers of all signs, whenever those signs are signs of identity and difference and the difference between identity and difference. The shibboleth test can now be understood as operative in, and indeed, constitutive of, any drama of covert signaling, on the one hand, or of policing and "passing," on the other, as narrative parsings of the "eggshell shibboleth of caste and color" have so often dramatized.[10] Shibboleth testing in this expanded sense processes dress, gesture, expression and attitude, the manifold, sometimes exquisitely subtle, signifiers of belonging or not-belonging—belonging or not-belonging to a class, a sex, a gender, a sexual orientation, a race or ethnic group, a profession, and on and on, from the most weighty to the most trivial and evanescent of the myriad and layered differentiations of social existence. In *Shibboleth: For Paul Celan*, Derrida offers powerful generalizations that reiterate, perforce and knowingly, this movement of inflation and idealization: e.g., "A *shibboleth*, the word *shibboleth*, if it is one, names, in the broadest extension of its generality or use, every insignificant, arbitrary mark, for example the phonemic difference between *shi* and *si* when that difference becomes discriminative, decisive, and divisive" (26). The political-theoretical claims that we offered in previous paragraphs follow a similar pattern: "the shibboleth," as the concept of itself, allegorizes the biopolitical capture of the body in language while opening political space as the friend/enemy distinction (though also, as will very shortly become clear, in ways irreducible to the Schmittean binary opposition)—all the while allegorizing its conceptual profligacy as a version of "metaphor in the text of philosophy." The semantic exfoliation of the word *shibboleth* in modern and contemporary English that we examined at the beginning of this book rehearses a similar tension. This word's constellation of meanings (test-word, password, slogan, cliché) suggests, we suggested (echoing a great Benjaminian phrase turned slogan or cliché), the waning of the logos in an era of technical reproducibility. The loss of meaning that the word *shibboleth* means is a hermeneutically generative matrix. One does not need to propose large politico-theoretical allegories in order to tap these energies; any reading of the story in Judges runs into hermeneutic questions that cluster around the shibboleth test. Presumably a different test-word with the *shin* phoneme might have been chosen; why this one? Who would not want to linger over the word *shibboleth*'s double meaning of grain and stream, bread and water, the fundamentals of life, despite the evacuation of these meanings (along with any others that philology might someday disinter) at the moment of crisis and crossing? And how—to reprise the question that closed this essay's previous section—might the story of the shibboleth test be read in conjunction with the murderous and self-destructive turns of Jephthah's acquisition and exercise of sovereignty?

The semantic and thematic lure of the shibboleth may be understood in conjunction with its mechanical repeatability—its deadly force as border control technology—by way of Derrida's quasi-concept of iterability. As the "concept of the possibility of ideality" yet also of "the limit of all idealization," iterability signifies the co-implication of repeatability and alterity: "It entails the necessity of thinking *at once* both the rule and the event, concept and singularity."[11] Iterability at once opens the possibility of idealization as the repetition of the same, and alters, displaces, and renders impure the effects of plenitude that are generated. This difficult, powerful line of thought accounts both for the production and circulation of meaning and for the mechanical repeatability of technique, both of which intertwine in the shibboleth. If the shibboleth were pure, self-identical event, it could not become a concept and would not function as a *test*; it would have neither significance nor effectivity as a technique of identification and border control. This doubling and infinite redoubling of "the" shibboleth is remarked in the very drama of the test: it is a demand to *repeat*, and repeat in the mode of the *same*. A felicitous performance consists in the repetition of the word *shibboleth* as the "same" word (within the range of a "native speaker": the same, that is, across variations of voice, tone, timber, even across accepted accentual variation, accepted mistakes, accepted "bad grammar," and so on: the same as recognized on the immaterial level of the phoneme and in concert with a myriad other signs, many of which can be non-linguistic, as "one of us"). Yet this effacement of difference in the production of identity (us, them, our language, their language) originates in repetition, and thus in a repeat*ability* opening the possibility of the empirically "first" utterance of the test-word as sovereign demand. The shibboleth test owes its concept, its wider significance, and its political power to its iterability. This means in turn, however, that, despite its ferocious ability to target and kill, the shibboleth works only insofar as it is able to miss its mark. The repeatability that makes it a weapon also exposes it to failure and errancy. On the one hand, as Rousseau affirms, there is no accent-free speech; on the other hand, the subtleties of an accent, like all other linguistic phenomena, are constituted by and vulnerable to replication. To the extent that self and other—the subject and the object of the sovereign decision—require the shibboleth test for their realization, they are under the sway of a "law of iterability" that "exceeds the intentional structure that it renders possible" (*Limited Inc*, 130). It will always be possible for an Ephraimite to pass the test or for a Gileadite to fail it. And of course the Gileadite giving the command and the example— "Say now, 'Shibboleth'"—can always choke on his word, demand a mangled sound, derail the test before it begins— not an implausible scenario after a few thousand repetitions have taken their toll (though of course the power asymmetry between test-giver and test-taker would lead to a different outcome if the former rather than the latter is mispronouncing the word). Such exceptions to the rule will then be ascribed to empirical contingencies (the Ephraimite is an exceptional mimic or had a Gileadic nanny; the Gileadite has a speech impediment, or his attention wanders, or the unconscious speaks); but exposure to such contingency forms a nonaccidental part of the rule. No mark, signature, or speech act can function except insofar as it can go wrong, misfire, be repeated, forged, or cited, otherwise and elsewhere. If the shibboleth test provides the only guarantee that the other is other, this guarantee is unguaranteed. The friend/enemy distinction can never be truly secured. (It is for this reason—to open a brief parenthesis, looking forward to a history that left its impact on Celan—that nineteenth-century Western European anti-Semitic writing tends to adopt an even more strident tone than usual when affirming, with, say, Gobineau, the "particular accent" of the Jew. Racist ideologies grow anxious in the proximity of linguistic identity tests and need to be ready to discount them, for although language, according to these ideologies, *ought* to be an expression of race, language is frustratingly permeable, reproducible, unreliable.)[12] The sovereign moment of decision and the Schmittean political space produced by the shibboleth test are both derivative of a deeper condition of insecurity, such that self and other cannot be constituted in a specular relationship without residue.

Hence the explosive aggressivity that characterizes the shibboleth story, as summed up by the Ephraimites' taunt and the Gileadites' reaction, and as given narrative expression by Jephthah's history and fate. Like a reaction formation, the story of the shibboleth test supervenes on the story of a quasi-illegitimate leader who, expelled from the community, owes his reintegration and his precarious sovereignty to a speech act: the promise sworn by the elders of Gilead before the Lord. Jephthah then supplements that speech act with another: a conditional promise made directly to God. The form of Jephthah's vow follows a conventional *do ut des* formula (reversal being equally conventional: if the Lord grants this, I shall do that), except in one regard: the vow registers, in the dangerous open-endedness of its offer of sacrifice, the infinite distance that a contract with God needs to span.[13] Mythic violence fills that space with the oathmaker's only child. The cost of (a brief spell of) rule as judge of the people is the barrenness and scattering—the castration and accelerated extinction—of a leader who will never be a patriarch. (In all these ways Jephthah is the pointed opposite of the ur-patriarch Abraham: Abraham, who has a son rather than a daughter, who obeys a dictate from God rather than proposing a contract, who evades child sacrifice, and whose seed, God promises, will multiply as the stars of heaven.) Commenting on the logic of sacrifice, Jacques Lacan suggests that sacrifice seeks to capture the Other in the circuit of desire, as though the gods desired as we do: "the sacrifice signifies that, in the object of our desires, we try to find evidence for the presence of the desire of this Other that I call here *the dark God*" (*Dieu obscur*)."[14] The dark God exacts the highest possible price, as he must; for the cruelty of his demand at once indexes and conceals the impossibility of knowing what or whether the Other wants. ("To what purpose is the multitude of your sacrifices unto me? saith the LORD: I am full of the burnt offerings of rams, and the fat of fed beasts; and I delight not in the blood of bullocks, or of lambs, or of he goats" [Isaiah 1:11].) Translating into the idiom being examined here, we could say that, at this point in the text, the name of God is the unpronounceable shibboleth that both underwrites and hollows out sovereign authority. The subsequent story of the shibboleth test repeats and displaces that pattern. The test produces a border that promises to be harder to cross than those crossed by a bastard son turned judge of the Gileadites; it transforms the ambiguous kinship of Gileadite and Ephraimite into a binary opposition maintained by a microscopic but knife-sharp difference; it makes space for a sovereign decision; it unleashes lethal, targeted violence. And it also undermines sovereignty and identity in ways we have only begun to examine.

The shibboleth test recodes the sublime distance between God and humanity as the arbitrary difference between a voiceless postalveolar fricative and a voiceless alveolar fricative (*shin* and *sin*). It transforms the unpronounceable name of YHWH, the Tetragrammaton, into a "secret without secret," as Derrida puts it (*Shibboleth*, 26): a secret without semantic or theological depth, a prohibition without content and in that sense without epistemological, mythological, or psychological dignity. The secret as shibboleth, the secret that leverages and weaponizes the depthless unconscious of linguistic competence, is nothing more than the linguistically inscribed body's ability to pronounce a word. No conscious knowledge or intent, no reserve of intelligence or virtue, no strength of character or will can access this fundamentally banal though, at the crucial moment, all-important secret-without-secret. It is accessed only when "the subject," however defined, does not know what it is doing. If death is the penalty for failing the test in the biblical story, this accords with the exemplarity of that story. Whether destined to be killed or to be allowed to cross over and live, the subject as locus of intentionality is annihilated in the very moment that it is being "subjected" in the sense of being produced as a target of sovereign force. The subject occupying the position of sovereign power, though protected from the threat of immediate physical death, suffers an equivalent annihilation *qua* subject as it cites or repeats a test-word that it does not know how it knows how to enunciate, listens to a repetition that it does not know how it knows how to judge, and "judges" without the support of a center of will and identity. Nor is this subject properly "sovereign" even in its inaugural decision to open the sequence of repetitions through which the shibboleth test demonstrates its murderous power, as tester and test-taker play out their preprogrammed if never completely predictable roles. Language irrevocably contaminates sovereignty, as Derrida and others have stressed: "A pure sovereignty is indivisible or it is not at all, as all the theoreticians of sovereignty have rightly recognized, and that is what links it to the decisionist exceptionality spoken of by Schmitt. This indivisibility excludes it in principle from being shared, from time and from language. . . . Sovereignty withdraws from language, which always introduces a sharing that universalizes."[15] The sovereign decision composing the shibboleth test, enabled not just by the empirical circumstances that have created a power differential between two opposed yet hard to distinguish groups, but—also and therefore—by unchosen linguistic differences into which it has always already been thrown, and in and through which it comes into existence as speech act, is radically exposed to the linguistic contingency that it instrumentalizes. Only because it is thus contaminated and exposed can it perform itself as an instrumentalization of linguistic difference. If we call the deciding instance at the origin of the shibboleth-test-enabled bloodbath "Jephthah," as many summaries of the story do—though he is not mentioned in the relevant verse—we are left with an antonomasia for a disorder internal to all claims to and expressions of sovereignty and identity in language. It is perhaps telling that Jephthah—previously so prone to give speeches and perform speech acts—disappears during, or into, the account of the shibboleth test per se. And if we do allow his name to linger on in this scene, we might wish to give a little extra spin to the two etymologies that (possibly) entwine in the name Jephthah (better transliterated as Yiphtah), via a verb פתח (*patah*) that means not only to open (the womb, but also the mouth, eyes, ears, and so on, and thus: to speak, see, hear, and the like) but also to bore through, carve, or engrave. To open, to go through, to write: as the improperly proper name of the shibboleth test, this judge's name opens as a mark that cuts itself apart.[16]

Subjectless and meaningless in the space of its event, the shibboleth has in itself no aim, no purpose or telos, despite the measureless stakes it puts into play. It is not even certain that, in this context, "shibboleth" remains a *word*. The test bears not on a full word, not even on an entire word stripped of its semantic value, but only on a piece of that skeleton, the *shin* phoneme with which it begins. The Ephraimite who fails the test fails it in the first instant of utterance, at the first hiss of the *s*; the ax falls there, before the rest of the word can arrive. The hiss is an orphaned bit of a word; a Joyce can trope it as verbal excrement ("Shitbroleeth," murmurs Leopold Bloom, recalling "vaguely the past of Ephraim" but at least getting the opening fricative right, in the Circe episode).[17] Cut off as it is from lexical or morphological or semantic context at the moment of the test, this fragment is neither one coherent thing in itself (for it is exposed to judgment) nor part of a whole (for only here does the shibboleth-test obtain its grip). And this fragmentary fragment or fragment of a fragment is not even necessarily a phoneme; its difference from mere noise shades toward illegibility. It could be a gasp, the intake or expulsion of a (last) breath; flatulence; background noise. No longer securely speech, this hiss-fragment no longer insulates its "speaker" from animality or even from inanimateness. It is *taken* as language, but that inevitable taking-as-language simply records the exposure of the sovereign decision to the undecidable. The sovereign decision occurs in and as a fractured moment of madness. Yet if in a sense this phoneme-noise-fragment is not enough language, in another sense it is too much language: it could belong to any number of languages; the *sh* or *s* of the test-taker—or whatever phoneme, phone, or allophone one imagines as the secret of *shin* or *samekh*—could be headed toward some completely different, unheard-of language. These uncertainly linguistic particles perform their difference—the deadly difference between Gileaditic and Ephraimitic, languages so similar that, it seems, they cannot otherwise be distinguished; languages that are and are not "one"—but they perform this difference only because they can wander elsewhere. The shibboleth story therefore underscores another insight that Derrida elaborated out of a web of quasi-concepts such as the trace, dissemination, and iterability: "No such thing as *a* language exists." Babel not only scatters languages and humanity, it fragments language internally, because the unity of a language, as understood by classical linguistics, is a "unity . . . open to the most radical grafting, open to deformations, transformations, expropriation, to a certain a-nomie and de-regulation."[18] Hence the tightly paradoxical double affirmation that Derrida offers in *Monolingualism of the Other*: "We only ever speak one language—or rather, one idiom, only"; "We never speak only one language—or rather, there is no pure idiom" (8). A word like *shibboleth*, for instance, can cross linguistic borders, perhaps not entirely unscathed but living on nonetheless, as a loanword or what in German is called a *Fremdwort*, a stranger in a strange language, the beneficiary of unforeseeable and uncontrollable acts of hospitality. And a word like *shibboleth* ("if it is one," as Derrida remarks more than once [*Shibboleth*, 26]) can, *as* "shibboleth," point to itself as the name of a nameless self-alterity, while enacting this alterity as it crumbles into pieces, into phonemes and letters that in turn can always have unpredictable itineraries and effects. In *shibboleth* there is babel, which is also to say deconstruction: "If I had to risk a single definition of deconstruction, one as brief, elliptical and economical as a password, I would say simply and without overstatement: *plus d'une langue*—both more than a language and no more of a language."[19] Which is also to say, in yet another Derridean idiom, in *shibboleth* there is haunting; for this sovereign technic raises ghosts that no checkpoint ("Stand and unfold yourself") can control ("*Barnardo*: Tis here. *Horatio*: Tis here. *Marcellus*: Tis gone").[20]

The word (or "word") *shibboleth* is a catachresis for a remainder or crypt: a fractured fragment cut off from its word and from the Word, from meaning, intention, or aim—from the very performativity it enables. Because it "marks the multiplicity within language, insignificant difference as the condition of meaning" (*Shibboleth*, 28–29), it is language in not being securely language. It is metaphor as the effacement of the blankness of an uncertain crossing. Only as such a blind fragment can it be weaponized. This stub is the condition of possibility of *shibboleth* as the word that unleashes sovereign power; shelters the ethnos; purifies the family line; affirms "nativity" in and as language; distinguishes friend from enemy and *this* language from *that* language; draws and polices a border; targets and kills; folds back on itself to become the concept of this technic. With each cut, it marks with difference and finitude the sovereign instance and identity it so efficiently serves. One could say that this shibboleth-death, this secret without secret, silent as the "c" in the trigraph *sch* with which French and German render in writing that perilous fricative, is a name for the unpronounceable name of God if one is going along with a remark that Derrida risks in "Des Tours de Babel": "the proper name of God (given by God) is divided enough in the tongue, already, to signify also, confusedly, 'confusion.'"[21]

## 4

## *Schibboleth*

Derrida

The poetry of Paul Celan, difficult, powerful, and unyieldingly committed to finding paths for poetry in the wake of the Holocaust, has inspired a vast but often pious and scholastic critical archive. Inevitably, much scholarly labor has been devoted to tracking down topical references, a task that often uneasily counterpoints the formal or hermeneutic or rhetorical analysis that critics have also sought to bring to Celan's work. Peter Szondi's famous commentary on the late poem "Du liegst im großen Gelausche" ("You lie amid a great listening") offers an exemplary conjoining of close reading and biographical contextualization, the latter enabled by Szondi's own memories of Celan's visit to Berlin in December 1967. Szondi firmly rejects the notion that "a knowledge of the real-life referent" can "itself constitute an interpretation"; such knowledge rather "gives us access to the history of the poem's genesis," and his essay sets out to "retrace the process of . . . crystallization" that resulted in a poem.[1] A degree of unresolved tension, however, remains between the critic's expert close reading of "the poem as a tissue of words" and his illuminating account of the "coincidental, external precondition" (Celan's visit to the Plötzensee prison and to a Christmas market; his having been lent a book on the murders of Rosa Luxemburg and Karl Liebknecht; his having been shown the Eden Hotel where Luxemburg and Liebknecht were beaten nearly to death before being murdered) "that made possible the poem's concretization in words" (*Celan Studies*, 91). In *Shibboleth: For Paul Celan*, Jacques Derrida honors Szondi's ability "to bequeath to us the irreplaceable passwords of access to the poem, a priceless *shibboleth*"; but like Szondi he affirms that even "left to itself without witness," the poem would still "speak":

> Szondi was the first to acknowledge this. He set this enigma before himself with an admirable lucidity and prudence. How is one to give an account of this: concerning the circumstances in which the poem was written, or, better, concerning those which it names, ciphers, disguises, or dates in its own body, concerning whose secrets it partakes, witnessing is *at once* indispensable, *essential* to the reading of the poem, to the partaking that it becomes in its turn, and, finally, *supplementary, nonessential*, merely the guarantee of an excess of intelligibility, which the poem can also forego. *At once* essential and inessential. This *at once* stems—this is my hypothesis—from the structure of the date.[2]

The date, both as a concept and singular inscription (in the case of the poem that Szondi is interpreting, an effaced date, "Berlin. 22./23. 12. 1967," that Celan had included in a first published version but later omitted) offers Derrida an important point of entry—a shibboleth—for his commentary. Celan's writing extends hospitality to this approach, both in the complex forms of attention his poems so often pay to dates and dating, and in his hardly less complex reflections on poetry and dating in his Büchner Prize acceptance speech, *Der Meridian* (1960):

> Perhaps one can say that, in every poem, its '20th of January' remains inscribed (*daß jedem Gedicht sein "20. Jänner" eingeschrieben bleibt*)? Perhaps the novelty of poems that are written today (*heute geschrieben werden*) is precisely this: that here the attempt is most clearly made to remain mindful (*eingedenk*) of such dates?
>
> But do we not all originate (*schreiben wir uns nicht her*) from such dates? And which dates do we attribute to ourselves (*schreiben wir uns zu*)?[3]

These not quite rhetorical questions, which are cast emphatically as questions of poetic writing (*einschreiben, schreiben, hinschreiben, zuschreiben*), form part of the central statement of *Der Meridian*, aspects of which will engage us in the next section; for the moment, a short gloss suffices. The "20th of January" refers back to Celan's quotation of the first sentence of Georg Büchner's novella *Lenz* earlier in his speech: "Lenz, who 'on the 20th of January went through the mountains'" (der 'den 20. Jänner durchs Gebirg ging') (194/179). This quotation from Büchner offers an extra layer of complexity as regards dates and dating. When *Lenz* was first published, its opening sentence read simply: "Den 20. ging Lenz durch's Gebirg." In including the name of the month, Celan follows the lead of the standard scholarly edition in his day, which added "January" in the dialect form "Jänner" to Büchner's opening sentence on the basis of contextual evidence.[4] Yet this minor supplement resonates when Celan reiterates it: January 20 is the date of the Wannsee Conference in 1942, the lakeside meeting at which the Nazi leadership committed itself to genocide.[5] January from Janus: two-faced god of portals, doors, and gates; here, a figure as double-edged as the shibboleth, mechanism of passage and blockage, election and extermination. Celan leaves the reference to the Holocaust unspoken: a certain keeping-silent forms part of the task of remaining "mindful (*eingedenk*) of such dates." He folds his own work into the date "20. Jänner" at this point, gesturing toward his recently written prose piece "Gespräch im Gebirg," "Conversation in the Mountains" (1960) ("where I had a person walk, 'like Lenz,' into the mountains"), and quoting lines from the "Stimmen" sequence in his recently published collection *Sprachgitter* (1959):

> Stimmen vom Nesselweg her:
> *Komm auf den Händen zu uns.*
> Wer mit der Lampe allein ist
> hat nur die Hand, draus zu lesen.

> Voices from the nettle-path:
> *Come on your hands to us.*
> Whoever is alone with the lamp
> has only his hand to read from.

Celan italicizes the second line of the quatrain when he cites it in *Der Meridian* to signal an affinity with a phrase from Büchner's text on which he reflects at various points in the speech: Büchner's dryly bizarre description of Lenz (Büchner's fictional Lenz, that is) finding it sometimes disagreeable that he could not walk on his head ("Nur war es ihm manchmal unangenehm, dass er nicht auf dem Kopf gehen konnte"). Celan's poem transforms *gehen* into *kommen* and head into hands: the voices summon the addressee toward a nettle path to be walked, excruciatingly, on one's hands. Adjacent to this summons, the quatrain pairs an axiom about reading. The painful way onward is perhaps to be read off and out of the hand, as a transmission from hand to hand (we shall reencounter this motif in Celan's poem "In eins"): a hand that signals the *written* word, providing a figurative analogue of the *schreiben*-cluster of self and date that Celan elaborates in the passage cited. "In each instance I started to write from a '20th of January,' from my '20th of January,' I encountered . . . myself" (201/184). Writing here may be called the *experience of the date*, if, like Philippe Lacoue-Labarthe, we take the word *experience* "in its strict sense—the Latin *experiri*, a crossing through danger," and "avoid associating it with what is 'lived,' the stuff of anecdotes."[6] Or, put a little differently: the value of anecdotes about Celan visiting Plötzensee or the Eden Hotel lies in their ability to alert us to an experience constituted as a *written* trace in a poem. As trace—as crossing or dating—the experience is no longer either simply contingent (the lure of the anecdote) or simply necessary (the lure of aesthetic form), and it no longer belongs to a self except through and as an essential estrangement. In *Der Meridian*, at a point in the text to which we shall need to return, Celan calls the "I" of such ex-perience "an—estranged—I" ("ein—befremdetes—ich") (194/178–179). This is the I of commemoration and anticipation—of the date from and toward which the I writes itself (*herschreiben, zuschreiben*).

Derrida elicits an aporia constitutive of the possibility of dating. In dates, as in signatures, the unrepeatable—the singular trait—repeats, divides, and recedes from readability in becoming readable. In order for a date to be legible it must suspend the "unique marking that connects it to an event without witness" (15). The date withdraws in appearing *as* date. Yet—and, Derrida suggests, this is what yields "the chance for the poem's exclamation"—the date does not simply negate itself in a "generality" (say: the totality of historical time within which it is would be an infinitesimal, negated and sublated point); rather, it effaces itself before "another date, the one *to which* it speaks, the date of an other, masculine or feminine, which is strangely allied in the secret of an *encounter*, a *chance* secret, with the same date" (9). The date is thus a "future anterior" (25), split between an irrecuperable past and an uncertain future (the uninsurable future of a promise, including that of terror, as Derrida's reflections on "9/11" were to stress, a decade and a half after this text on Celan).[7] This analysis, which represents yet another exfoliation of Derrida's analysis of iterability and the aporetics of the mark, also means that a date is always already the loss and commemoration of itself. Exposed to chance and loss ("it is always possible that there may no longer be any witness for this witness" [32]), it exists as division and displacement.[8] Hent de Vries suggests that the seemingly circular return of the date is therefore best troped as an ellipsis (a word that, like its cousin *ellipse*, stems from the Greek *elleipsis*: falling short, leaving out): "A date is elliptical when it does not come back and when, far from being a *hic et nunc*, it is from its very inception divided, doubled, tripled, or even further multiplied within itself."[9] Gathering together as quasi-concepts poem, shibboleth, and date, Derrida writes of the poem as the *partage* of a secret-without-secret: "What the poem marks, what enters and incises language in the form of a date, is that there is a partaking of the *shibboleth*, a partaking at once open and closed. The date (signature, moment, place, gathering of singular marks) always operates as a *shibboleth*. It shows that something is not shown, that there is ciphered singularity" (33). And this open but reticent singularity is a multiplicity and a gathering. "What if there were more than one thirteenth of February?" Derrida asks, addressing his question to a date in a Celan poem that we shall shortly be trying to read. "Not only because the thirteenth of February recurs, becoming each year its revenant, but above all because a multiplicity of events, in dispersed places—for example, on a political map of Europe, at different epochs, in foreign idioms—may have come together at the heart of the same anniversary" (21).

A date, therefore, is never one with itself. Here it will be useful to open a parenthesis and circle back for a moment, as promised, to Faulkner's *Absalom! Absalom!*; for although Derrida's reflections on dating in *Shibboleth* bear on poetry and particularly on Celan's poetry, those formulations draw on the great rethinking of writing announced in *Of Grammatology*, where it is demonstrated that "all graphemes are of a testamentary essence."[10] In Celan, the ethical and poetic burden of that testamentary element is so weighty that the risk to which his language exposes itself can seem to disappear into the speaking silence of the poem. When Celan co-signs "20 Jänner," he inscribes at the heart of his literary task a trace of the catastrophe that, in his Bremen Prize acceptance speech (as we shall see later in more detail) he had named minimally as a happening (*Geschehen*) for which language gives no words. But the testamentary imperative has to endure at every point the uninsurability of the graphic mark. Internally split and ahead of and behind itself, a date can be effaced, forgotten, repressed, displaced, counterfeited. Its "politics" are not prescribed.[11] The scene in *Absalom! Absalom!* that we glanced at earlier, in which "the eggshell shibboleth of caste and color" seems ambivalently and momentarily to shatter at an interracial touch, becomes even more complex when read in connection with the most fantastic gesture performed by this hallucinatory novel: its foreclosure of the Haitian Revolution of 1795–1804, in and through the story of Thomas Sutpen's self-fashioning. Narrated at multiple removes, riddled with obscurities, but datable to the 1820s by the fiction's historical grid, Sutpen's story has him making his way to Haiti after his ur-trauma of being turned away from the front door of a grand Virginia house by a black slave. Of the story's many mysteries (how he got there, how he learned French, and so on), the most salient, according to the text's chain of narrators, is not how the barely educated young man got from "a rotting cabin in Virginia" to employment as a sugarcane field overseer in Haiti ("because that did infer time"), but "how he got from the field, his overseeing, into the besieged house when the niggers rushed at him with their machetes"—a crossing over that "seemed to have occurred with a sort of violent abrogation of time which must have been almost as short as his telling about it—a very condensation of time which was the gauge of its own violence."[12] At the climax of this formation-story, Sutpen exits the besieged house and mysteriously "subdues" the rebellious blacks by exposing his white skin and deploying his white willpower:

> "Not how he did it. He didn't tell that either, that of no moment to the story either; he just put the musket down and had someone unbar the door and then bar it behind him, and waked out into the darkness and subdued them, maybe by yelling louder, maybe by standing, bearing more than they believed any bones and flesh could or should (should, yes: that would be the terrible thing: to find flesh to stand more than flesh should be asked to stand); maybe at last they themselves turning in horror and fleeing from the white arms and legs shaped like theirs and from which blood could be made to spurt and flow as it could from theirs and containing an indomitable spirit which should have come from the same primary fire which theirs came from but which could not have, could not possibly have. . . ." (210)

Left unremarked in this feverish scene (a fantasy redolent of the worst sort of bad faith: flesh being made "to stand more than flesh should be asked to stand" is of course the very condition to which slaves, not overseers and plantation owners, are exposed)—left unremarked is the question of what is going on in this fictional Haiti, during a year that the novel dates as 1827. Has the Haitian Revolution been effaced, displaced, and defeated by Sutpen's superhuman will? Or, as John T. Matthews suggests, is Sutpen deluded to think that he works for a white French plantation owner rather than for a light-skinned Haitian, a so-called *jaune* who has profited from the revival of racial hierarchies in postrevolutionary Haiti?[13] Sutpen and his narrators seem to believe (or at least pretend to believe, perhaps thereby deriving a little phantasmatic compensation for the defeat of 1861–1865, the wound around which much of *Absalom! Absalom!* turns) that the revolution has not yet happened, and perhaps even that it never quite ever happens (Sutpen "saved" the "whole place" "as well as the lives of all the white people on it" [217]). But either way, Sutpen gets both his fantasy and his comeuppance: he marries the plantation owner's daughter, only to abandon her when he finds out she is part black, though not before having with her the son who will ruin his subsequent effort to found a white patriarchal line in Mississippi (this is Charles Bon, who passes as white, gets engaged to his half-sister Judith, and is shot by his half-brother Henry). The essential point to retain in the present context is that Faulkner has balanced the eggshell shibboleth of caste and color on a date that encrypts and phantastmatically effaces the Haitian Revolution—the great slave revolution that haunted the antebellum American South—precisely to the extent that Sutpen imagines the occupants of the "besieged house" as *white*—and thereby self-fashions *himself* as white. For to turn away from being turned away at a fine front door is to turn away from being *not*-white. The very passage from "field" to "house" carries the touch of an American slave narrative. The novel multiplies the cracks in the eggshell. Sutpen's face resembles "pottery" when he first appears in Mississippi (26); and although a little later his adaptable skin will evolve toward an "honest sunburn" (37) as he swindles land from the Chickasaws and builds a house "even bigger and whiter than the one he had gone to the door of that day" (215), his whiteness, such as it is, disappears into "black" descendants (a grandson, Charles Etienne St. Valery Bon, who reads as white; a great-grandson, Jim Bond, who, because of his dark-skinned mother, reads as black: the line descends from *bon* to bondage).[14] When Rosa runs without moving and halts without stopping in the "eggshell shibboleth" passage, she replays not just Sutpen's primal scene of being blocked by a black slave but also Sutpen's subsequent, phantasmatic crossing-and-not-crossing the color line as he crosses from field to house "in a very condensation of time which was the gauge of its own violence." And when, much later in the novel's plot, a much older Rosa runs once again into the by now crumbling Sutpen mansion, suffers once again the touch of an elderly Clytie, but this time strikes her hand away and—if that were not enough to repress the resonance of that earlier, world-shaking touch—knocks her to the floor "with a full-armed blow like a man would have" (303), she accedes to a door behind which Henry is dying, "yellow" from disease (306), his skin (like that of "saddle-colored" Jim Bond) forwarding a final trace of the Haitian detour. The encrypted date that is "Haiti" in *Absalom! Absalom!* gathers to itself, as threat and promise, the potential illegibility of the shibboleth of race.

Rosa's full-armed blow parallels a deadlier transformation of touch into cut, late in the novel. At the end of his extraordinary career, Thomas Sutpen is sliced down with a scythe wielded by Wash Jones, an employee whose daughter he has insulted, and the novel goes to some lengths to reactivate the figure of the "touch" ("*'Stand back. Don't you touch me Wash.'—'I'm going to tech you, Kernel'*" [154]). The touch of the shibboleth is necessarily and radically ambivalent, and the promise of redemption that this touch brings will always also be doubled by the threat of a murderous cut.[15] We are thus led back to Derrida's meditations on Celan. For the date is already being thought as a mark and a cut—shibboleth being "what enters and incises language in the form of a date." The figure of circumcision becomes the second focal point that Derrida uses to plot his ellipse around the word *shibboleth*. Like the date, circumcision happens "only once" even as it suggests a certain repetition and return (in the ringlike cut of male circumcision; in the word that names this procedure, at least in languages like French and English that use the Latinate term for it—this particular ring-motif, it must be said, serves Derrida's text more as figure than argument). Circumcision is shibboleth as incision and inscription, a writing on the body that marks admission to a community and the assignation of a name. In its literalness as a bodily cut, circumcision may at first seem distant from the ambiguities we have been parsing; yet precisely as *inscription* it is also always already figurative, spiritualizable (a displacement that "does not date from Saint Paul: it is not limited to the circumcision of the soul or the heart," Derrida comments [55], thinking perhaps of the command Moses relays in Deuteronomy 10:16: "Circumcise therefore the foreskin of your heart, and be no more stiffnecked"). It is translatable to the point of being "defin[ed] . . . only at the limits of definition, of limitation, of circumscription itself" (59). And though the literal word *circumcision* (*Beschneidung*) appears rarely in Celan's writing, "by contrast, the *tropic* of circumcision disposes cuts, caesuras, ciphered alliances, and wounded rings throughout the text" (54). Such cuts are reading-wounds that solicit readings that go as deep as the depthless inscription itself (Derrida draws for his commentary on a line from Celan's "Dein vom Wachen": "Sie setzt/Wundgelesenes über": it carries/the wound-read across). Reading is wounding and wounded because the mark, the shibboleth or secret-without-secret to be read, grants access only in retreating, such that reading is driven "to the quick, to the point of bleeding," in Derrida's vivid trope (54). As Michael G. Levine comments, "If such wounds may be said to be illegible, they are so not merely in the sense of being resistant to reading but in the way they inexhaustibly demand it."[16]

The poem is a wound that wounds: it "enters and incises language in the form of a date," leaves its mark on language, composes itself as and exposes itself to "the *double edge* of a *shibboleth*": double because, as "the mark of a covenant or alliance," a shibboleth "also intervenes, it interdicts, it signifies the sentence of exclusion, of discrimination, even of extermination" (63). A certain inversion structures Derrida's argument: the poem, which speaks only in holding in reserve the unspoken and unspeakable, owes its living on to the unpronounceability of its shibboleth—the very characteristic that grants a shibboleth, in an appropriate political context, its murderously efficient (if never entirely reliable) force. That paradox remains on the edges of Derrida's discussion, for though he stresses the poem's exposure to the "terrifying ambiguity of the shibboleth," his wide-ranging essay tends not to examine in detail the specific ways in which Celan's texts address that ambiguity. There remains the broad question of the poetic destiny, so to speak, of this loaded word. We have seen how powerfully the word-turned-concept "shibboleth" expands outward from the biblical narrative to become an available figure for the opening of agonistic political and biopolitical space and the actualizing of sovereign decision; for the very possibility of semiotic systems ("the word *shibboleth*, if it is one, names, in the broadest extension of its generality or use, every insignificant, arbitrary mark"); for the technologies—always potentially lethal technologies—of policing, filtering, surveillance, privatization, encryption, and decryption that along ever-accelerating trajectories saturate the regime of modern technics. Followed down that line of its snowballing course, "shibboleth" intersects the domain of what Celan called *Doppelzüngigkeit*, doubletalk, and *Kulturkonsum*, cultural consumption: techno-speech, commodity-speech, slogan, and cliché, the opposite of poetry as the *schicksalhaft Einmalige der Sprache*, the fateful singularity of language. Those comments of Celan's, which form the core of a short note he sent to the French bookstore Librairie Flinker in 1961, in response to a question about bilingualism in poetry, deserve closer inspection in this context:

> I do not believe there is such a thing as bilingual poetry [*Zweisprachigkeit in der Dichtung*]. Doubletalk [*Doppelzüngigkeit*]—yes, this you may find among our various contemporary arts and acrobatics of the word, especially in those which manage to establish themselves in blissful harmony with each fashion of consumer culture [*Kulturkonsum*], being as polyglot as they are polychrome [*genauso polyglott wie polychrom*]. Poetry—that is the fateful singularity of language [*Dichtung—das ist das schicksalhaft Einmalige der Sprache*]. Hence never—allow me this truism: poetry, like truth, goes all too often to the dogs—hence never what is double [*Also nicht—erlauben Sie mir diese Binsenwahrheit: Dichtung sieht sich ja heutzutage, wie die Wahrheit, nur*

*allzuoft in die Binsen gehen—also nicht das Zweimalige*].[17]

Celan published very few prose statements, and none were intended to be read effortlessly. His ironic signing-off with a *Binsenwahrheit*, a cliché, about *Dichtung* going, like *Wahrheit, in die Binsen*, to the dogs or down the drain (literally: in the rushes), may be read as a hint that, despite appearances, the *Einmalige* and the *Zweimalige* might, to cite a much-cited phrase from Wordsworth's "Essay upon Epitaphs" (1810), have "a finer connection than that of contrast." It is a *Binsenwahrheit* that true *Dichtung* is not *Binsendichtung* (*sit venia verbo*); yet perhaps the fateful singularity of the poem consists precisely in holding itself open, in a certain way, to repetition. Perhaps poetry as *das schicksalhaft Einmalige der Sprache* is sometimes fated to cite other texts and attune itself to broadcasting; and perhaps sometimes the fate of *Zweisprachigkeit* is best avoided when a poem welcomes into itself "other languages." These are not forced paradoxes; they relay obvious aspects of Celan's poetic practice. The word *Schibboleth*, when it appears in Celan, triggers particularly intense concatenations of languages and citations. Derrida's privileging of the word *shibboleth* ("if it is one") in his first major text on Celan and his affirmation that "in a language, in the poetic writing of a language, there is nothing but *shibboleth*" (33), encourage us to take a close look at how the poetic writing of this particular poet has cut, dated, or circumcised this (un)word.

# 5
# Schibboleth
*Celan*

The word *Schibboleth* appears in two poems of Celan's: "Schibboleth," from *Von Schwelle zu Schwelle* (1955), and "In Eins," from *Die Niemandsrose* (1963). We know from Celan's correspondence that he had the biblical story well in mind when he was writing and titling the earlier poem.[1] Yet both this poem and the later one offer a peculiarity of which neither Derrida nor, to my knowledge, any other reader has made public note: in these texts, the word *Schibboleth* does not appear either to mean or function as a test-word in the ordinary sense. Drawing on semantic resources that we saw Hegel and Marx exploiting, Celan could be said to be using this word in a way proximate to the English "slogan," though that suggestion offers no more than an initial spur to reflection. Even on a hasty first reading it is clear that both poems are providing more than one possible referent, in more than one language, for the singular noun *Schibboleth*, a word that appears once in each poem: in the fifth stanza of the poem titled "Schibboleth":

> Ruf's, das Schibboleth, hinaus
> in die Fremde der Heimat:
> Februar. No pasaran.

> Call it, the shibboleth, out
> into the foreignness of the homeland:
> February. No pasaran.

And in the first stanza of "In Eins":

> Dreizehnter Feber. Im Herzmund
> erwachtes Schibboleth. Mit dir,
> Peuple
> de Paris. *No pasarán.*

> Thirteenth of February. In heart's mouth,
> awakened shibboleth. With you,
> Peuple
> de Paris. *No pasarán.*

Ignoring for the moment numerous complexities, taking these stanzas in isolation, and stressing only the most obvious syntactic cues, we may say (as discussions of these texts inevitably do) that in the earlier poem the word *Schibboleth* appears to refer to "Februar" and to "No pasaran," and in the later one to "Mit dir,/Peuple de Paris," to "*No pasarán*," and possibly backward to a date, "Dreizehnter Feber" (which may also be read descriptively, as the date of the shibboleth's awakening, and/or narratively, as the cause of the awakening). (The syntactic reference backward in the first poem to the contracted "es" of "Ruf's" will be discussed later, along with other modalities of the word *Schibboleth*'s self-referencing in these texts.) These fragmentary exclamations vary in specificity. The dates "Februar" and "Dreizehnter Feber" ("Feber" is the Austrian dialect form of "Februar") conjure various possible historical events. Both can be taken to reference the Austrian civil war of February 12–15, 1934, when Engelbert Dollfuss's troops crushed the socialist movement as part of his establishment of Austrian fascism during his brief tenure as dictator; the heaviest fighting was on February 13.[2] But that is only one referential or commemorative vector. Although "Dreizehnter Feber" is more referentially restricted than "Februar"—it cannot, for instance, relay more than a faint echo of the February revolutions of 1848 in France and of 1917 in Russia, since these broke out late in their respective Februaries, not at all close to the thirteenth of the month— the specificity of this date, aided by the metonymic proximity of "Mit dir, /Peuple/de Paris" (a phrase conjuring various political moments from the French Revolution to the Paris Commune and beyond), opens at least two other commemorative possibilities.[3] The first and most obvious, a topical reference at the time when "In Eins" was being written and published, would be to the public funeral, attended by hundreds of thousands of mourners and protesters, of nine victims of police violence on February 13, 1962, in Paris; they had been killed during demonstrations on February 8 against the OAS and its brutal efforts to prolong the Algerian war.[4] The second—more distant, but not at all far-fetched, given the thematic importance of acts of transmission and mediation in this poem—would be to the massive antifascist demonstration of February 12, 1934, in Paris, via its mediation in the left-wing press the next day, when several papers ran banner headlines offering a French equivalent of the Spanish phrase toward which both of these poems are underway: "Le Fascisme ne passera pas!"[5]

"No pasaran" / "*No pasarán*," "they will not pass," is certainly the most slogan-like of these heaped-up shibboleths (if that is what they are): slogan-like not (or as much as possible not) in the sense of *Kulturkonsum*, of hackneyed or commodified speech, but in the sense of a testamentary affirmation, pledge of allegiance, and memorable, pithy rallying cry. This Spanish phrase, which became the watchword of the Republican forces and particularly of the defenders of Madrid, was the leitmotif of the famous speech by Dolores Ibárruri Gómez, broadcast over the radio on July 18, 1936, the day the generals declared their revolt and the war began. Celan brings the notion of "shibboleth" here to a dramatic reversal of its biblical role, for rather than winnowing would-be passers-over who are being forced to utter it aloud, this shibboleth unites its speakers against an enemy who intends to force a pass in defiance of that shibboleth. (When Franco took Madrid in 1939, he reportedly offered the annihilating rejoinder: *Hemos pasado*, "we have passed.") It is worth qualifying a little Derrida's description of the phrase "*no pasarán*" as "in sum, a kind of Spanish shibboleth, a password, not a word in passing but a silent word transmitted like a symbolon or handclasp, a rallying cipher, a sign of membership and a political watchword."[6] Political watchword to be sure; password and "silent word"—yes, in the context of the poem "In Eins," as we shall see, that gloss will become relevant. But one should first stress the fact that, in the context conjured up by Celan's repetition of this phrase, *anyone* can, *everyone* is being actively encouraged to repeat or cite this shibboleth: it is being sent over the radio in hopes of further media uptake; even Franco's forces and his fascist allies are welcome to acknowledge it and agree with it, or at least repeat it and send it along. Echoing a well-known French slogan from the Battle of Verdun ("*ils ne passeront pas*") that, as noted, had been repurposed by the Left in its battle against fascism in France in the 1930s, "*no pasarán*" eschews national and linguistic chauvinism. This shibboleth, loyal to international socialism, welcomes all accents, all pronunciations. And indeed, Celan, in the poem "Schibboleth," offers the written equivalent of a mispronunciation by dropping the acute accent over the final syllable of the verb. The missing accent accentuates the point.[7] The slogan "*no pasarán*" offers figurative passage, through its mediatization, to an extended community of political solidarity, but it does not weaponize nonsemantic linguistic elements in the service of border control. Rather, the shibboleth here semantically negates the probing operation of technologies of testing. The enemy, unspecified in this historically quite specifiable phrase, is neither essentialized (no one *has* to be a fascist), nor subjected to an identification-test mechanism. Tests for entry into or exit from the city may well be needed; hard-to-identify enemies, hiding and doubling as the self, may well exist (and indeed, the Nationalists boasted of their fifth column within Madrid); but as far as this shibboleth is concerned, membership in the community is in principle open to anyone willing to affirm that they, the fascists, shall not pass. The speech act harbors the utopic possibility that "they" not pass because no one is a fascist any longer. It limns the fantastic promise of itself being the ultimate password (here we touch on one of Derrida's intuitions that we noted earlier), giving a "pass" to those who speak it, allowing them to pass over precisely because they affirm that the fascists who seek to pass over will not pass. Its verb is in the future tense, not the imperative (they *will* not pass, not they *shall* not); it holds history open to a futurity from which fascism is excluded. Its affirmation endures past the fall of Madrid.[8] "*No pasarán*" deconstructs the drama of the shibboleth, at once reiterating it (for indeed, "they will not pass" could be said to be the very motto of a shibboleth test) while reversing its charge (the deadly threat now originates from those who wish to pass over, not from those holding the fords of the river), and deracinating it from the constraints of the linguistically encoded body, from the crushing positivity of history, and from all calculations of border control. The fact that fifth-column fascists can mouth its words is not its concern. It does not target and test, and it has no self-protective mechanism; its refusal is sheer affirmation, promise, and prayer.

This blend of defiance and openness helps explain both why *"no pasarán"* became and has remained—particularly when kept in Spanish—a rallying cry of the left, and why Celan's poems put this phrase into dialogue with the word "Schibboleth." "*No pasarán*" would be the shibboleth of a politically committed yet radically open community: committed in its opposition to those who would destroy its openness, open to the risks posed by that very openness. It would be a community *à venir*, hospitable to unforeseeable solidarities, encircled by a border that is also a non-border, and that its shibboleth affirms without policing (refusing to "do" the blocking-off that it "says"). It would be a transnational, multilingual, mass-mediated community, the opposite of a Burkean "little platoon," a fascist state, a Nazi *Volk*. Yet it would always also remain exposed to these and other political threats, both ideologically, insofar as its need to defend against its fascist other reintroduces versions of sovereign violence and exclusion; and pragmatically, insofar as the fascists may "pass" (in whatever sense, and as they literally did). If it retains its utopic thrust, it also bears the imprint of these threats. The iterability that the phrase *"no pasarán"* underscores as it commits itself to the radio waves renders it, like all language, exposed and finite. Appropriated from a French nationalist-militaristic context first by French and then by Spanish antifascists, it remains vulnerable to reappropriation, mimicry, and failure; broadcast by a doomed republic, it comes down to us as an infelicitous speech act in its particular historical moment. Like "Dreizehnter Feber," it records damage. If, in its future tense, *"no pasarán"* continues to promise resistance to fascism, it is thanks to incisive, but always singular and finite, acts of recollection and reaffirmation, as in these two poems by Celan, both of which place this famous phrase at the culminating point of narrative movements that are implied, in the earlier poem, by its call to "call out" its "Schibboleth," and, in the later poem, by its characterization of its "Schibboleth" as "erwacht," "awakened," but also—awakening an old resource, a transitive meaning of *erwacht*—"awaited," "keeping watch for": *erwachtes Schibboleth* as the shibboleth to come, the messianic word, the depthless secret in the *Herzmund* that holds it in vigil.[9]

These poems thus present themselves as political acts of memory and address, at the same time that, like all literary texts, they disable the reduction of language to message, or form to meaning—that would be one quite traditional way to reformulate Derrida's claim that "in the poetic writing of a language, there is nothing but *shibboleth*." And since these poems stage their poetico-political affirmations by way of a foregrounding of that burdened word, we touch on fundamental interpretive issues when we ask what it means to call "das Schibboleth, hinaus/in die Fremde der Heimat"; what an "erwachtes Schibboleth" is; why this awakened, awaited shibboleth is not simply in the mouth, but "im Herzmund." Inextricable from those questions are others we have been brushing up against: What is a shibboleth if it is not a test-word? What would a shibboleth be if it is (or: "is") many different words and phrases from different languages? And if, in these poems, the word "Schibboleth" refers to certain other words and phrases in these poems, as syntactic prompts and conventions of metonymic proximity and thematic congruity suggest, and if those words and phrases convey a political engagement, how may we read that engagement together with the complexity and polyvalence of a poetic statement that at once demands, undermines, and withdraws from referential and semantic judgments? For as we already intuit, even on the basis of the two isolated stanzas quoted earlier, nothing in these texts guarantees that the word "Schibboleth" refers to any other word, including the word that it is (not) itself. The shibboleth could be everywhere or nowhere; it could be a phrase, multiple phrases, a poem, a word, part of a word, not a word—a "20. Jänner" that cannot be spoken, written, pronounced, known.

Some of these possibilities require more elucidation than others. The most immediate complication that readers of "In Eins" encounter is the proliferation of potential intratextual referents for the word "Schibboleth":

IN EINS

Dreizehnter Feber. Im Herzmund
erwachtes Schibboleth. Mit dir,
Peuple
de Paris. *No pasarán.*

Schäfchen zur Linken: er, Abadias
der Greis aus Huesca, kam mit den Hunden
über das Feld, im Exil
stand weiß eine Wolke
menschlichen Adels, er sprach
uns das Wort in die Hand, das wir brauchten, es war
Hirten-Spanisch, darin,

im Eislicht des Kreuzers "Aurora":
die Bruderhand, winkend mit der
von den wortgroßen Augen
genommenen Binde—Petropolis, der
Unvergessenen Wanderstadt lag
auch dir toskanisch zu Herzen.

*Friede den Hütten!*

IN ONE

Thirteenth of February. In heart's mouth,
awakened shibboleth. With you,
Peuple
de Paris. No *pasarán*.

Little sheep to the left: he, Abadias,
the old man from Huesca, came with his dogs
over the field, in exile
stood white a cloud
of human nobility, he spoke
us the word that we needed into the hand, it was
shepherd-Spanish, in it,

in the ice-light of the cruiser "Aurora":
the brotherly hand waving with the
band taken from the word-large eyes—Petropolis, the
wandering city of the unforgotten, lay
also for you tuscanly on your heart.

*Peace to the cottages!*

From its opening date to its final exclamation, the poem pivots around its "erwachtes Schibboleth," without allowing any word or phrase in any of its many languages (German, dialect German, French, Hebrew, Spanish, Russian, Latin, Greek, along with an unexemplified reference to "shepherd-Spanish") to claim authority as *the* keyword of passage.[10] The first stanza offers the resonant polyglot fragments that we were examining above; the second stanza tells the story of the transmission of "the word that we needed"—a pithy description of what, conventionally understood, a shibboleth is—through the figure of Abadias, a shepherd-messenger. The first half of the third stanza enters the figurative interior of this word: "darin," "in it," shines the ice-light of the

"Aurora," and in that dawning, enlightening light, the brotherly hand waves the blindfold that has been removed from eyes that a "word" has enlarged. In its second half, after the dash, the third stanza addresses an interlocutor in second-person singular familiar, as Celan's poems almost always do; these ciphered lines become easier of access if readers are able to hear in "Petropolis" an allusion to the poet to whom the volume *Die Niemandsrose* is dedicated, Osip Mandelstam ("toskanisch," which grafts a German adverbial ending onto a Russian word for nostalgia, *toska*, reinforces the allusion to Mandelstam, who puns on this word).[11] The poem then closes with a truncated version of the famous motto of Büchner's incendiary pamphlet *Der Hessische Landbote* (1834), "Friede den Hütten! Krieg den Palästen!" ("Peace to the cottages! War to the palaces!"), a phrase that inverts and translates a French Revolutionary saying, "Guerre aux châteaux! Paix aux chaumières!," and that, like "no pasarán," has had a significant afterlife as a leftist slogan.[12] The utterances "Mit dir, /Peuple/de Paris," *"no pasarán,"* and *"Friede den Hütten!"* (the latter two italicized presumably to mark their status as citations) are the most obvious candidates for shibboleth-as-slogan, but they are by no means the only politically inflected references. Abadias is in exile from Huesca, the city that the Republicans tried disastrously to take in 1937; the "Aurora," radiating the cold light of its name within the "word that we needed," is the cruiser that, with a blank gunshot, signaled the assault on the Winter Palace that began the October Revolution in 1917.

If we then ask what principle of selection is guiding this convocation of political events, distilled out of a century or so of European history and spread geographically "like stars all over the map of Europe," as Derrida comments (*Shibboleth*, 24), one answer is that the poem is recasting the biblical story of intertribal violence as European revolutionary struggle. All of the poem's major allusions invoke historical moments of revolution, protest, or politically determined civil war (Austria in 1934; Paris in 1789, 1848, 1871, 1934; the war in Spain; the October Revolution). The shibboleth, reclaimed from its role as murderous sovereign technic, would be the watchword of anticapitalist and antifascist struggles that, despite their international character, inevitably take the form of civil war in national contexts. A reading of "In Eins" that pressed the poem toward a thematic statement would fairly conclude that it pledges allegiance to a pan-European socialist humanitarianism in the context of a developed capitalist modernity (arguably joining its commitment to revolution to a politics of nonviolence, through its focus on the "brotherly hand" and its excision of the second half of Büchner's phrase). In the same spirit of ideological assessment one could note certain cultural presuppositions: the self-consciously patriarchal inflection of the poem's story of the word's transmission; the self-consciously European frame of reference in which this inheritance occurs.[13] An overall account of the poem's political stance would likely deem it Eurocentric, cosmopolitan, socialist-revolutionary and egalitarian (the "word that we needed"—the shibboleth of shibboleths, perhaps—goes unspecified except in one respect: it is a humble dialect-word, "shepherd-Spanish").

Such an assimilation of "In Eins" to a political statement, a recognizable attitude or position (or set or mix of attitudes and positions), nameable within a modern Western political vocabulary and locatable here and there on a prefabricated political spectrum, cannot simply be avoided, any more than the targeting force of shibboleth technologies can simply be neutralized—or (to recall the other face of iterability) any more than a phrase or slogan, even when spoken from the heart or held in the *Herzmund*, can be insulated from the reproduction, circulation, and consumption that exposes it to what we saw Celan calling *Kulturkonsum*, and to the risk of becoming what the English language is able to call, pejoratively, a "shibboleth."[14] Yet typecasting ascriptions of this sort efface all too rapidly the singularity of a literary text—the text as "language as form and direction and breath" (*Der Meridian*, 194/178)—and thereby cause us to overlook the ways in which this poem is offering its political affirmations *as* poetic form and address. One would draw closer to the spirit of such thoughtful poetry by noting how the text prods us to ask, for instance, whether "peace to the cottages" does not demand an excision of palaces if such peace is genuinely to be thought at all—a demand that registers here as a poetic act of excising: an *active* inheritance of Büchner that would itself be erased if readers translate and thematize the partial erasing of the citation as a banal pacifism. The text honors the singularity of certain moments in the history of European liberationist struggle by inscribing tokens of them—in some cases much-cited tokens—in a poem that seeks to be in-one without synthesis. Thus it is that the poem's various exclamations and citations both do and do not refer to the "erwachtes Schibboleth." We asked earlier what a shibboleth would be if it were not a test-word. Derrida's reflections on *shibboleth*, which relieve this word-turned-concept of its consignment to instrumentality, are concretized in a poem in which the word "Schibboleth" at once proffers itself as a keyword and withdraws from meaning. "Schibboleth" would be the "word" *of* this insistence and withdrawal of the word: the word that shares and divides, enacting the aporia of a path or passage that exists in refusing itself, cutting across languages and language, and across itself as word. To be *erwacht* in this context is to affirm such ex-isting, "at the edge of itself," as Celan described the stance of a poem ("das Gedicht behauptet sich am Rande seiner selbst") (*Der Meridian*, 197/181). It is to be at the edge of time:

to be awakened to awaiting the shibboleth-to-come. This shibboleth is at most quasi-conceptual, and the dramatic exclamations that accompany it make their political wager *as* affirmations of such open reserve. The affirmations and commemorations of socialist struggle remain affirmations and commemorations: this poetic reserve is not an aestheticism. Each phrase is exemplary, and none is an example; none is *the* shibboleth (as a theater of sovereign violence would demand). The narrative at the center of the poem allegorizes this reserve or secret as the story of the handed-over word, the "word that we needed" that is spoken and transmitted "into the hand": spoken into the poem itself, rather than into a space of represented speech (these are presumably the lines that Derrida had in mind when he was describing "*no pasarán*" as "a kind of Spanish *shibboleth*, a password, not a word in passing but a silent word transmitted like a *symbolon* or handclasp").[15] The word *Schibboleth* at once offers itself and withdraws from the phrases, citations, and narratives that would deliver semantic content. These phrases, citations, and narratives proffer singular gestures of memorialization and commitment in solidarity with each other and in affirmation of the "erwachtes Schibboleth," coming together *in eins* in the linguistic event of openness and reserve that we call a poem. "The uniqueness of the poem, in other words, yet another date and *shibboleth*, forges and seals, in a single idiom, in eins, the poetic event, a multiplicity of languages and of equally singular dates" (Derrida, *Shibboleth*, 29). In a somewhat more overtly political register, drawing on reflections by Jean-Luc Nancy and others, one might think of "In Eins" as performing a literary thinking of "communism without (substantive, determinate) community": a communality as distant as possible from the sovereign authority and violence epitomized by the fasces.[16]

Drawing on a different though related vocabulary, Levine persuasively links this poem's gathering of dates and citations to Benjamin's notion of the constellation. The poem "does the work of the historical materialist described by Benjamin, blasting certain moments out of the course of history. It does so in order to bring them into another kind of alignment, to make them revolve not only around a particular date but also and above all around each other" (22). Such a constellation—an in eins, not a Sein—will also need to be thought as an address and an encounter. We approach here a point of deep affinity between Celan and Derrida, both of whom tirelessly hold their writing open to the event, the other, the time of the other, and the arrival of the other-to-come; and it is appropriate here to return, if all too rapidly and inadequately, to Celan's dense reflections on poetry in *Der Meridian* that were touched on earlier. Structuring his remarks around a handful of scenes and sentences from texts by Büchner, Celan proposes that literature (*Dichtung*) breaks at a certain point with mimetic art. Literature "must travel the path" (193/178) of imitative and formally or mechanically determined art ("Art, you will remember, has the qualities of the marionette and the iambic pentameter" [187/173]); but the literary moment is one of rupture: a "step" and an "act of freedom" (189/175): not mere self-forgetting (which would be akin to the clean formality of the marionette) but a "place where a person succeeded in setting himself free as an—estranged—I" (195/179). There is a deathly quality to this estrangement: invoking Büchner's Lenz, Celan writes that his setting-himself-free is "a terrible silence" that "robs him—and us—of breath and speech [*es verschlägt ihm—und auch uns—den Atem und das Wort*]" (195/179). There follows the famous sentence: "Literature: that can signify a breath-turn [*Dichtung: das kann eine Atemwende bedeuten*]." Perhaps,

Celan continues (the text unfolds here, in an intense sequence, under a repeated "perhaps"), perhaps here the mimetic force of language shrivels; perhaps an estranged I is set free; perhaps an Other is set free; and perhaps the poem here assumes its identity, mindful of its unique "20th of January" (196/180). Without pretending to do justice to these stunningly daring formulations, we may recall that the difficult freedom they describe consists in a remaining-mindful (*eingedenk*) of a double-edged date—consists, that is, in an attentiveness that would be historical, ethical, and political in being poetical. The rupture with representational and instrumental language constitutes an inscription that leaves the poem open to history and to the futurity of an encounter. Christopher Fynsk offers the valuable comment that Celan challenges "the thought of finitude and historicity that Heidegger pursued in the existential analytic, because [Celan] thinks singularity *always in relation*."[17] Thought itself, along with the "I," differs from itself in thinking a being-with that is always already, in its singularity, toward and open to the other. And such poetic thinking is a remaining-mindful of a date. For it cannot be overemphasized that the "date" here is an event, not an empirical positivity; it is as much *à venir* as marked by pastness; it is the mark of the other as event, as event-as-other, as other-event, at once singular and spectrally multiple. The poem hopes "to speak *in the cause of an Other*—who knows, perhaps in the cause of a *wholly Other* [*vielleicht in eines* ganz Anderen *Sache*]" (196/180, Celan's italics). The poem heads for an Other, and its *Atemwende* is also an *Atempause*, attentiveness as a cut or caesura in breath:

> The poem tarries or stops to catch a scent [*verweilt oder verhofft*]—a word to be referred to a creature—when confronted with such thoughts.

No one can say how long the pause in breath
[*Atempause*]—the stopping to catch a scent and the
thought [*das Verhoffen und der Gedanke*]—will
continue [*noch fortwährt*]. (196–197/180)

The poem pauses like a wild animal (*verhoffen* is a term from
venery: the animal pauses to listen or catch scent) at the
thought of the other that it seeks, toward which it is underway. As Derrida puts it in his own, slightly different idiom:
the poem orients itself toward a singular yet undetermined
other-to-come, unknown, monstrous, messianic, addressing
itself "to the stranger, to the other, to the neighbor, to the
guest, to whomever" (*Shibboleth*, 56). A radical hospitality is
implied in this stance, as is a humility inseparable from the
largest of claims. Literature undermines aesthetic ideologies, for it represents a "radical calling-into-question of art
[*In-Frage-Stellen der Kunst*]" (192–193/177). And the literary
moment of freedom calls into question all sovereignty, for
it acknowledges only "the majesty of the absurd [*Majestät
des Absurden*]" (190/175).

One way to approach a poem such as "In Eins" in the light
of such questions is to attend to its complex use of pronouns.
The poem opens and closes with addresses to a singular,
familiar-form "you" in the dative ("Mit dir"; "lag/auch dir toskanisch zu Herzen"). In this poem, rather atypically for
Celan, there is no "ich"; the speaker, from the beginning *in
eins* as a plurality, seems to partake of a "wir" ("seems"
because as will be reviewed momentarily, the "wir" that flick-
ers into view in the poem's tenth line remains grammatically
recessive). Coming after the invocation "Mit dir/Peuple/de
Paris," the poem's "wir" potentially includes that "dir," though
it does not simply incorporate it: the invocation remains an
address, a claim of community ("*mit* dir"), not a grammatical
or narrative subordination or incorporation of one pronoun

into another. These pronouns, furthermore, are separated by the poem's turn to a third person, the emphatic "er" that precedes the proper name "Abadias" and launches the text's narrative of encounter and transmission. And this "er"—or rather, its reiteration: the stanza's second "er"—pushes the first-person plural, when it finally appears, first into its dative form, and then into a dependent relative clause ("er sprach/uns das Wort in die Hand, das wir brauchten"). No pronoun in the poem occupies an unmediated position of utterance. The first stanza is a burst of verbless sentence fragments; the second and third stanzas form one long anacoluthonic sentence that begins as a fragment ("Schäfchen zur Linken," a phrase that reverses the right-left sorting of sheep and goats in Revelations: these are not saved sheep), and then launches into a narrative split grammatically into three disjointed parts, the first subject-verb construction ("er, Abadias . . . kam") interrupted by a different if presumably appositional subject-verb unit ("im Exil/stand weiß eine Wolke/menschlichen Adels"), before picking up again with another "er"-plus-verb construction, in which the plural first person makes its brief and subordinated appearance ("er sprach/uns das Wort in die Hand, das wir brauchten"); more grammatical disjunctions articulate the sentence through its conclusion at the end of the third stanza. Both at the beginning and at the end of the poem, the subject who addresses the "du" is fundamentally indeterminate: not a continuous or coherent subject; certainly not a lyric subject in a post-Petrarchan or post-romantic sense. The phrase "im Herzmund," modeled on the common German expression *im Volksmund* ("in the vernacular"), should be read not as the expression of a felt interiority but as a passion of language — let us say: a passion of and for that in-heartmouth-awakened word of words *qui n'en est pas un*, "Schibboleth."[18] And the "du" addressed by this nonsubject is at once singular, collective, and mobile. Pressed into the dative in both of its appearances, first by a preposition ("mit dir") and then by a verbal construction ("lag dir"), this "du" fails to appear as a subject, either in the grammatical sense (which would require the nominative case) or in traditional philosophical, psychological, or political senses; it remains as distanced from lyric utterance as the "wir," and never congeals into a unified addressee. The two instances of "dir" have different rhetorical orbits, which are quite hard to conjoin.[19] The second "dir" can be referred plausibly to an extratextual referent (Mandelstam) and somewhat more awkwardly to an intratextual one (Abadias, the word-bearing *angelos* and guardian of memories of revolution);[20] the first "dir," though tied appositionally to a specific collective noun, forms part of an apostrophe that derives its energy from line breaks that emphasize not just the leap into French, but the unsecured movement of poetic language, as the poem pauses and quests for its other in and through its address to the other: "Mit dir,/Peuple/de Paris."

The poem, from a place haunted but not controlled by a plural pronoun, addresses an other that is at once singular and multitudinous. It addresses but does not, in a conventionally lyric sense, *speak* to that other: no lyric consciousness or coherent dramatic persona underwrites the trope of voice. Voices proliferate and speech occurs; but the act of speaking, cut by a voiceless line break ("er sprach/uns das Wort in die Hand") is a handing over that inhabits yet also exceeds patriarchal transmission, filiation, inheritance. Pluralities address pluralities, *in eins* but not *vereint*, *vereinigt*, or *geeinigt*, with no subject controlling any point of origin, from the opening date stamp to the final fragmentary citation extracted from an unsigned pamphlet of plural authorship.[21] This radically heterogeneous collectivity or constellation is here the very the condition of politics, and for that matter of culture and memory. It is also a singularity: a poem, an address, a date, a death, a word. A word that withdraws from pronunciation not as part of a test but—through a difference that can neither be stabilized nor effaced—as the opening, or cut, of a poem. The proliferating line breaks marking the macaronic affirmation "Mit dir, /Peuple/de Paris" offer an insistent reminder of the irreducibility of language to pronunciation, to language-testing, to "language" as ontic entity or ideal totality (e.g., Saussurean *langue*), let alone as an index of identity, an ethnic marker, a calculable resource, a realization of sovereign power. No test will pinpoint this "dir"; no pronunciation can control this "/Peuple/". As Kristina Mendicino comments in a searching study of Celan's practice of citing, echoing, and troping on texts in *Der Meridian*, "the already-heard turns into the unheard."[22] The cut, circumcision, or spacing that (de)composes this collective cannot be subsumed under a preset rhythm or assimilated to linguistic or nonlinguistic forms of identity, though it can be approached by way of the breath-turn, *Atemwende*, and its figure, apostrophe.

# 6
# "S(ch)ibboleth"
*Apostrophe*

Like "In Eins," and for that matter like many of Celan's poems, the poem titled "Schibboleth" has rarely garnered sustained attention, despite the extra international visibility it acquired via Derrida. The main vectors of Celan studies have passed through different texts—understandably enough, given the power and difficulty of the oeuvre overall, and the gravitational draw of the major poems (and though "Schibboleth" will be granted a certain exemplary status here, I shall not be claiming that it is a major poem).[1] Derrida's short book, for its part, offers relatively perfunctory commentary on the poem that its title names and reiterates (a reiteration lodged, as we know, in an echo chamber of references):

> Inserted in the second line of "In Eins," the word *shibboleth* forms the title of a longer and earlier poem, published in 1955 in the collection *Von Schwelle zu Schwelle. Shibboleth* could also serve, by metonymy, as the title of the collection. Indeed, it speaks of the threshold, of the passing of the threshold (*Schwelle*),

of that which permits one to pass or to go through, to
transfer from one threshold to another: to translate.[2]

Having granted exemplary status to this text, Derrida rapidly
notes similarities between "In Eins" and "Schibboleth": "One
finds there more or less the same configuration of events,
sealed by the same February anniversary, the linking of the
capitals, Vienna and Madrid, substituting perhaps for the
linking, in 'In Eins,' of Paris, Madrid and Petropolis." More
intriguingly, he points to "a play of resemblances and differences, the *shibboleth between* the two poems":

> The two poems beckon to one another, kindred,
> complicitous, allies, but as different as they can
> possibly be. They bear and do not bear the same date.
> A *shibboleth* secures the passage from one to the other,
> in the difference, in the interior of the selfsame, of the
> same date, between Februar and Feber. They speak,
> in the same language, two different languages. They
> partake of it [*ils la partagent*]. (31)

The poems share and divide the unshareable and indivisible;
"ils partagent l'impartageable," as one can say in French, leveraging, in the spirit of *shibboleth*, the double meaning of
*partager* (to share, to divide: one could say divisively sharable—
which is to say translatable—as the German *Mit-teilung*, the
English im-parting).[3] A poem is a singularity, not a unity, but
there is an extra sense in which this particular poem, "Schibboleth," is not "one" poem: it beckons to another poem to
come, a poem that, even after Celan wrote it, remains a poem-
to-come for this poem—as it, from the past, remains a poem-
to-come for "In Eins." (And of course there are other sharply
marked transfers, translations, and crossings. Celan deliberately placed "Schibboleth" across from another poem about
giving and failing to give a word, "In memoriam Paul Eluard,"

in *Vom Schwelle zu Schwelle*, and allowed the phrase "in eins" to resonate in the poem that follows "In Eins" in *Die Niemandsrose*, "Hinausgekrönt."[4] But we shall simply follow here, in plodding fashion, the furrow of our privileged word.) A close look at the earlier text can hope to trace more concretely a line of intertextual entanglement, one that will eventually encourage us to return to Derrida's evocative suggestion that these poems intertwine as a poetic act of translation.

## SCHIBBOLETH

Mitsamt meinen Steinen,
den großgeweinten
hinter den Gittern,

schleiften sie mich
in die Mitte des Marktes
dorthin,
wo die Fahne sich aufrollt, der ich
keinerlei Eid schwor.

Flöte,
Doppelflöte der Nacht:
denke der dunklen
Zwillingsröte
in Wien und Madrid.

Setz deine Fahne auf Halbmast,
Erinnrung.
Auf Halbmast
für heute und immer.

Herz:
gib dich auch hier zu erkennen,
hier, in der Mitte des Marktes.
Ruf's, das Schibboleth, hinaus

in die Fremde der Heimat:
Februar. No pasaran.

Einhorn:
du weißt um die Steine
du weißt um die Wasser
komm,
ich führ dich hinweg
zu den Stimmen
von Estremadura.

SHIBBOLETH

Together with my stones,
the ones grown large with weeping
behind the bars,

they dragged me
into the middle of the market
over there
where the flag unfurls to which I
swore no oath whatsoever.

Flute,
double flute of night
think the dark
twin redness
in Vienna and Madrid.

Set your flag at half-mast,
memory.
At half-mast
for today and forever.

Heart:
make yourself known here too,
here, in the middle of the market.

> Call it, the shibboleth, out
> into the foreignness of the homeland:
> February. No pasaran.
>
> Unicorn:
> you know of the stones,
> you know of the waters,
> come,
> I shall lead you away
> to the voices
> of Estremadura.

Less compressed than later poems of Celan's tend to be, "Schibboleth" has the look of a relatively conventional post-romantic lyric. Not only does an "I" seem to be grounding the text, both as a character in a narrative and as a lyric subject of utterance, but the poem also appears to unfold according to traditional patterns of figurative inversion, moving its speaker from passivity to activity, from disempowerment to engagement, and from imprisonment to freedom or at least escape—from being dragged by others ("schleiften sie mich") to leading an other away ("Einhorn . . . komm, / ich führ dich hinweg"). The opening first-person narrative is followed by four apostrophes in four stanzas, each with its own narratively elaborated imperative. Each stanza features potentially difficult allusions and sharply compressed movements, but the poem's formal symmetries, controlled rhythms and chanting musicality appear to promise, at least on a first reading, an *invitation au voyage* that an aesthete need not hesitate to accept. It will of course come as no surprise to discover that this seductive clarity is misleading. The poem's title has signaled as much: "Schibboleth," a word we have learned to treat gingerly, suggests that the text it names is exposing itself to risk, and that readers will find themselves, despite, perhaps, some appearances to the contrary, "from the beginning *deported* [*verbracht*] into a foreign and strange region," as Peter Szondi comments in his famous study of Celan's difficult poem "Engführung."[5]

The condition of being *verbracht* is literalized in the dramatic first-person narrative of the opening two stanzas: "Mitsamt meinen Steinen,/den großgeweinten,/hinter den Gittern/schleiften sie mich. . . ." As always in Celan, the ciphered references are multiple and overlapping. The stones and bars evoke the poet's years in the Cernăuți ghetto and the Tăbărăsti labor camp, his parents' death in the Michailowka labor camp, and his crushing and lifelong survivor's guilt, while also reminding us more generally of the role of quarries and brickworks in the Nazi camp system, in which stone-breaking exemplified the policy of "annihilation through work," producing with ferocious rapidity broken bodies to be dragged away.[6] Stones, in Judaic tradition, are tokens of mourning and commemoration; and the poem may also be read as releasing here a reference to Niobe, whose petrification fails to put an end to her grief ("to this day tears trickle from the marble," *lacrimas etiam nunc marmora manant*: *Metamorphoses* 6.312). Furthermore, since, as we shall see in a little more detail later, Celan (like Mandelstam, though certainly very much in his own way) often associates stoniness with the poetic word, these stones that accompany the narrator in being dragged from a prison to an agora—a space of public life, display, torment, publication, oath-taking, political theater—suggest that a poet's language is being dragged into the open, with, *mitsamt*, the *mich* that in a sense is yet one more stone.[7] Unlike Niobe, however, whose tongue freezes to her palate, the narrator of "Schibboleth" remains able to deliver a cascade of speech acts. This self-dramatizing tone accounts in large part for the impression of a poem that is easy of access. There is a melodramatic cast to the narrative, and one gets the sense of a martyrdom being relished—a sense that grows stronger if one thumbs through early drafts of the poem, in which the narrator is hauled into the middle of the market, "wo die Galgen einst ragten/und heute/die Fahne sich aufrollt über/Schminke und Zukunftsgeswchätz" ("where the gibbets once loomed/and today/the flag unfurls over/makeup and prattle about the future"). Another draft mixes in the huzzas and drumrolls of a fascistic crowd: "inmitten des Jubels/inmitten des Trommelwirbels/rückten sie mich"; another stresses the narrator's fierce resistance to the flag: "[sie] entrollten die Fahnen,/der ich keinerlei Eid schwor/ (der ich den Haßeid geschworen/im Namen der stillen, der Sprache" ("they unrolled the flags/to which I swore no oath whatsoever/ (to which I swore the oath of hate/in the name of the silent, of language").[8] The narrative is minimal enough to leave open the possibility that the "I" is being persecuted as a member of a persecuted group (let us say: as a Jew); but the emphasis put on oath and flag encourages us to imagine him more as the hero and martyr of a political choice than as the victim of a racist shibboleth-machine. That interpretation gains further traction through details in the mini-narratives contained in the poem's subsequent apostrophes to flute, memory, heart, and unicorn: the twinned dark redness of fascist violence and crushed socialist resistance in Vienna and Madrid ("Februar" indexing, in the latter case, the relatively short-lived electoral victory of the Popular Front on February 16, 1936); the flag that memory is asked to strike to half-mast (a different flag, obviously, from that to which the narrator "keinerlei Eid schwor"); the shibboleth-proximate exclamations "Februar" and "No pasaran" that we examined earlier.[9] And if we take the somewhat idiosyncratic figure of the unicorn as a trope for poetry, self, and imagination, as internal and external cues might lead us to do, the narrator's shift from passive suffering to active leadership would begin to look like a transformation from political victim to poet-hero, or at least poet-survivor, leading literature away from the obscenities of the marketplace to the purity, or at least relative safety, of a dry, distant pastoral land (Estremadura, "extrema y dura").[10] Celan wrote to Gerhard Kirchhoff on January 15, 1964, that "Das Einhorn ist—auch—die Dichtung" ("the unicorn is—also—poetry") (Wiedemann, 728).[11] One of the drafts for this section of the poem also offers a hint in this direction by stressing that the unicorn cannot be bought and sold in the marketplace: "Nein, ihr erkaufts nicht, das Einhorn— /wie immer schreitet's einher/mit den Ziegen in Estremadura" ("No, you don't purchase it, the unicorn— /as always it paces along/with the goats in Estremadura") (*Werke*, 4.2, 186). Oriented toward aspects of the poetic self, the four apostrophes seem to offer ever-increasing claims of power. Flute, think shades of political solidarity and violence; memory, do not stop mourning; heart, call out the word of safe passage; unicorn, come, I shall lead you. The biblical creature that Martin Luther translated as *Einhorn* suggests deliverance, divine power, and danger;[12] and since in Celan's poem the *Einhorn*, whose name rekindles the opening stanza's symphony in *ein* (m*ein*en St*ein*en, /den großgew*ein*ten), knows all about the stones and waters of grief, memory, and poetic speech, it can easily be read as an avatar of the self and its suffering. Taking on a Mosaic role, the speaker would be proposing to summon and lead out of bondage, toward a promised land, the self itself as imaginative power—to summon and lead, that is, an element in the self that (the biblical resonances of *Einhorn* hint) cannot ordinarily be summoned or led.

Yet there is a counterpulse in the poem that ripples back through the heroic-masochistic narrative, deforming and estranging and hardening and vaporizing it. The stoniness of poetic language remains alien to the petrifying claims of representational art that Celan, echoing Büchner, associates with the figure of the Medusa's head ("perhaps at precisely this point the Medusa's head shrivels" and "an Other is set free"),[13] and is equally distant from the fullness and spontaneity of divinely guaranteed speech (as when Jesus invokes creation as hallelujah in the New Testament: "the stones will cry out" [Luke 19:40]). Stone is voice in its inseparability from silence and voicelessness; it is voice as the other of voice, the voice of the other, an other voice. To say that "language becomes lapidary, the poem has the character of an inscription [*Inschrift*]," as Celan does in a sequence of notes on stone that would repay exhaustive analysis, is to affirm a poetics very different from the reifying and theological idiom of aesthetic formalism.[14] The counterpulse can already be detected on the level of theme and image. The pastoral promise of the flute is reinflected by the flute's doubling into a *Doppelflöte der Nacht*: a double-flute that is not told to pipe ditties but rather to *think* a historical and political twinning, a doubleness of the singularity of the date: "denke der dunklen/Zwillingsröte/in Wien und Madrid."[15] Red Madrid and famously red Vienna ("das rote Wien," Europe's model for successful socialist governance from 1919 to 1934): two cities that are also, in the poem's lyric moment, bleeding under fascist takedowns—the poetic imperative to think this double-red-redoubled doubleness does not exclude the work of philosophico-political reflection (such reflection forms part of the imperative: "think"); but as a *poetic* gesture, it insists on the exposure to contingency indicated by the rhyme between the doubled medium and the redoublings of hope and catastrophe. Thus, through a linguistic transformation that no longer has a representational correlative, the flute (*Flöte*) becomes a redness (*Röte*), at which point the pastoral register opens onto politico-historical memories and geographies. The proposed flight to Estremadura, which on the level of dramatic monologue could appear either as the apotheosis of a sovereign poetic imagination or, in a more psychologizing vein, the defiant final escape-fantasy of a martyred visionary, now becomes a more complex movement toward "voices" attached to a toponym that, in the context of the Spanish Civil War, triggers memories of the massacre of Badajoz (Badajoz is the capital of the province of the same name, which forms the southern half of the autonomous community Estremadura in western Spain). Of the thousands killed after the city fell to the Nationalists on August 14, 1936, many were machine-gunned in the city's bullring: a killing zone that becomes a potential twin, a *Zwilling*, of the "Mitte des Marktes" to which the speaker has been dragged and from which he proposes to lead his addressee away—without, however, relieving memory of its imperative to set its flag at half-mast, "für heute und immer."[16] Celan's remarks about the "voices," in his two letters that discuss the poem, touch on pastoral and personal registers (to Chiva: "Rather oddly, the unicorn wished to let himself be led to the goats of Estremadura: a reminiscence, here renewed, of a flamenco that we heard at your place"; to Kirchhoff: "Estremadura is the Spanish Estremadura; the voices are—originally: at the time I had heard a Spanish song sung by Germaine Montero—shepherd voices [*Hirtenstimmen*]" [Wiedemann, 728]). But by replacing the *Ziegen* (goats) or *Hirten* (shepherds) of early drafts of the penultimate line with *Stimmen*, Celan opened the poem's pastoral and lyrical register to the voices of the dead, and the movement *hinweg* to figurative patterns that exceed representational parameters.[17] As we have seen before, the political force of the poem manifests itself precisely at the point where poetic language leaves mimetic representation behind.

For although, as this dimension of the text unfolds, the narrator remains open to heroic role-playing (and to self-parody, as the heroic act inflates to become a katabasis), the promise of a passing over to dead voices brings to legibility an irreducibly linguistic movement. No longer simply categorizable as a spatial indicator in a mimetic narrative or as a directional sign of imaginative transcendence, the adverb *hinweg* alerts readers to the chiming repetition of the adverbial prefix and suffix (and in the case of the preposition *hinter*, inseparable and in itself nonsemantic syllable) *hin*, a pattern that begins *hin*ter den Gittern, passes through the middle of the market, dort*hin*, and orients the final two apostrophes: the call for the shibboleth's calling out, *hin*aus, and the call for moving out the "ich" and the "Einhorn," *hin*weg. One may speak of a *hin*-movement throughout the poem, a movement unaffected by the lyric reversals of passivity and activity—so long as "movement" is understood as a motion or force irreducible to the spatiotemporal representational narrative that these various instances of *hin* enable: a movement of language *extrema y dura*, stony, alien, poetic. A few years later, in 1958, Celan was to orient the adverbial *hin* in this direction in his Bremen prize acceptance speech, describing language going through, *hindurchgehen*, the unspeakable (we shall take another brief look at that text in a moment); two years after that, in his great poetic statement *Der Meridian*, he would cite the final sentence of Büchner's fragment *Lenz*, "So lebte er hin" ("So he lived on") to relay the motion of *Dichtung* following but exceeding and rupturing the path of *Kunst*, and the motion of the step that releases "ein—befremdetes—Ich" ("a—made-foreign—I") (194 / 178–179). Caught up in this movement, the *ich*, rather than being a reservoir of heroic or lyric plenitude, is a disjointed I, disjointed in its foreignness and foreign in its disjointedness (marked in *Der Meridian* with a cluster of dashes: "ein—befremdetes—ich"), while the *Heimat* becomes *fremd* not just because of the fascist catastrophe but because *Heimat* names a sentimentalizing occlusion of a foreignness or movement no longer comprehensible in naturalistic terms.[18] The *ich* is the pronoun of the *hin*-motion that is the poem, a motion that opens toward a singular but indeterminable and interminable *du*, an other beyond telos or calculation, and beyond the distinction between the living and the dead. This *hin* as address as passage—the essential elements, let us not forget, of the biblical shibboleth story—may also be called writing: a writing that leaves a ghost-trace in the representational narrative as the doubling of *schleifen*, the strong verb that means to whet or grind (*schleifen, schliff, geschliffen*) shadowing the weak verb that actually appears in the text and that means to drag (*schleifen, schleifte, geschleift*). (An uncollected poem from the *Niemandsrose* period sharpens the *hin*-stylus thus in its opening lines: "Hin- und heraus-/geschrieben in/eine Hand—einen Himmel" [Wiedemann, 442].) Not just the dragging *dorthin*, to market, but also the call to call the shibboleth *hinaus* and the promise to lead the *Einhorn hinweg* become legible as figures for the figure of a trace-making force—a stylus that, whetted by stone and water, inscribes the questing and testamentary act that is the poem.

The figure of an address that moves *hin* is apostrophe: address as turning away, *apo-strephein*. Quintilian defines apostrophe as the trope of "addressing a person other than the judge," *sermonem a persona iudicus aversum*, and he recommends that it be used cautiously.[19] In poetics, apostrophe is the trope of addressing an absent, often dead, inanimate, abstract, or fictional entity. As Jonathan Culler comments in a seminal essay, apostrophe differs from other figures because it "trope[s] not on the meaning of a word but on the circuit or situation of communication itself."[20] In classical rhetoric, apostrophe risks *lèse-majesté* in turning away from the judge; in literary criticism, according to Culler, it inspires "embarrassment" as the privileged trope through which a lyric speaker lays claim to poetic tradition and to the vatic power to presuppose and create a responsiveness that in turn grants the speaker the very power that has been presupposed. In generating this circle of animation, apostrophe replaces narrative temporality with the present tense of address, and thus with a temporality that traditional literary criticism calls lyric immediacy and valorizes as transcendence: "its *now* is not a moment in a temporal sequence but a *now* of discourse, of writing" (168). Culler suggests that if, on the one hand, the figural "brazennness" of apostrophe generates unease because it threatens to make the "high calling of poetry . . . depend on a trope, an O," on the other hand this very figural excess indicates that when apostrophe "works," it does so by opening a text to "the uncalculable force of an event" (169). In the final pages of his essay, Culler moves his analysis beyond the parameters of voice, subjectivity, and will that habitually control critical discussion of lyric address. Recalling Paul de Man's reflections on the uncanny exchange between apostrophe and prosopopoeia—the trope of addressing the dead and the trope by which the dead speak—Culler, in one of the most remarkable moments in his distinguished career of writing about lyric, risks the claim that "we lose our empirical lives" when captured by the "apostrophaic time" of a poem such as Keats's "This Living Hand" (171).[21] The figure of address opens reading to the linguistic event of a "now" that would be radically finite, uninhabitable, unchosen, unclosed—in the idiom we have been exploring, the nonpresence-to-self of a poetic movement *hin*, toward the other, the other *of* address.

Celan's "Schibboleth" evokes the great classical and European lyric and apostrophaic tradition. The poem turns away—turns forever away, unlike Quintilian's rhetorician—from judge, jury, and hangman; abandons the narrative past tense; turns in order to address, in the lyric present of supplication, prayer, command and promise, an other, a plurality of others: others that at first appear to be others of the self, conjured up by a poetic self that is in turn conjured up by this other or these others: flute, memory, heart, unicorn. The heterogeneity of these addressees, which in ordinary parlance inhabit fundamentally different ontic regions (a crafted object; a faculty of mind; a body part turned metaphor for essential interiority and identity; a fantastic beast) signals the waywardness at the origin of poetic address. We have seen that a movement that initially appears as self-collection, as inward voyage turned outward turn, as reversal from passivity to activity, defiance to will, captivity to leadership, narrative to imperative to promise, becomes at every point a turn elsewhere, an opening that calls for a heart-giving that calls for the calling of the shibboleth, *hinaus*:

> Herz:
> gib dich auch hier zu erkennen,
> hier, in der Mitte des Marktes.
> Ruf's, das Schibboleth, hinaus
> in die Fremde der Heimat:
> Februar. No pasaran.

> Heart:
> make yourself known here too,
> here, in the middle of the market.
> Call it, the shibboleth, out
> into the foreignness of the homeland:
> February. No pasaran.

This apostrophe to the heart, the third in the sequence, at the heart of the poem, apostrophizes apostrophe itself as a giving (*geben*) and a calling (*rufen*). It is given to be known that the heart is to give itself to be known—to be recognized, to be exposed, to bear witness, to give itself as poetry as resistance at the center of fascist-capitalist power, in the middle of the marketplace, here at the middle of the poem. This giving-to-be-recognized is a calling out, in the second beat of the heart-apostrophe—although we may note that in this second beat, the addressee, "Herz," has dropped away and is now only implied: the first sign of a cut or circumcision that multiplies and intensifies as the poem calls out for the calling out of the poem's title word, the word of words that is never quite just a word, "Schibboleth." This word splits and appears before itself as the hysteron proteron of its own proleptic pronoun, the "es" sliced down to the "'s" of "Ruf's." The German language distinguishes between rhetorical apostrophe, *die Apostrophe*, and apostrophe of elision, *der Apostroph*, though the etymology in both cases is the same (*apostrophos*: the mark that records that a letter has been turned away from, i.e., omitted). At this extraordinarily dense point in Celan's stony text, the poem "Schibboleth" jams together address and elision as it calls for the calling out of its own name, its title, "Schibboleth"—or rather, what might be, what can always be, but what can always also not be its own title or name (for nothing can guarantee that "das Schibboleth," the shibboleth that is needed, is "Schibboleth"). The apostrophe to the (elided) heart calls for the calling out of a word that arrives before itself and arrives not itself at all: a pronoun apostrophaically elided to "'s": elided, that is, to the deadly sibilant that, in the biblical story, the shibboleth-test exists to conjure as the phoneme it excludes. *Schibboleth* is also, always already, this: 's, the sibilant of exposure. The poem insists: the s of its circumcised or castrated "es" repeats itself again in the definite article, "das," where the terminal s jams up against the initial *sch* of *Schibboleth*. "Ruf's, das

Schibboleth . . ." (with a final voiceless alveolar sibilant to close the phrase: "hinaus"). Before the shibboleth can arrive, the poem marks itself as exposed, in and as the hiss of the Ephraimite; it enacts the great epigram that Celan was to write some years later, in another language that was also his and not his (though differently): "La poésie ne s'impose plus, elle s'expose".[22] The poem calls for a calling out that is a choking on shibboleth, a choking on *the* shibboleth, *das* Schibboleth, whatever it might be, including the concept of itself ("the" shibboleth). The poem inscribes *itself* in this choking, this traffic jam of *s* and *sch*, of Ephraimite and Gileadite, for, although we can never be sure that the title "Schibboleth" is what is being asked for as "das Schibboleth," we can never not inscribe that title in the place held by this reiterated word; therefore, the poem's call to call out "das Schibboleth" in the middle of the marketplace and the foreignness of the homeland is always also: "Ruf's, das [Gedicht] 'Schibboleth' hinaus. . . ." The *Zwillingsgedicht* or double-poem of "Schibboleth," "In Eins," passes through this *point de capiton*: that poem's sentence fragment "Im Herzmund/ erwachtes Schibboleth" grants to "erwachtes" the role of jamming an s-hiss into "Schibboleth," a line in which, of course, "Schibboleth" (the word) must always also be readable as "'Schibboleth'" (the title of that poem; the poem of that title); readable, that is, as "Im Herzmund/erwachtes [Gedicht] 'Schibboleth'." The folding-in is also a folding-out, open to another and other date, time, text (Derrida's text, for instance, "das [Buch] 'Schibboleth' . . . ." as it opens itself to the poem). This elision-apostrophe of elision-apostrophe as poetic act as call to the other is the *Atemwende*, the breath-turn, the breath-cut, the ex-ha(i)ling through which the possibility of an other *shibboleth* is named. Performing this breathless cut, these twinned poems mark the *hin*-movement that also undergirds the mass-reproducibility, each time once and for all, of callings out that assume political responsibility only in and through such exposure. This too is the language of stone: the spelling-out of an other shibboleth, one that vibrates through the keywords *Steine* and *Stimme* (spelled *s*, normatively pronounced *sch*), through every *s*, *sch*, *z*, and *ß* in "Schibboleth" or in "In Eins," or elsewhere in Celan or in any other textual space open to its broadcast. Here the lyric-heroic *ich* and the various permutations of the reflexive *sich* scramble into the *s-c-h-i* of a *S(ch)ibboleth* that also encrypts and suspends within it the signature Ant*sch*el, the name that the poet anagrammatized (via the Romanian spelling Ancel; in Romanian the *ce* letter group is pronounced *tsch*) to Celan (the initial phoneme pronounced "s" in French, "ts" in German, "tsch" in Romanian). The reading imperative "Ruf's, in eins, Celans 'Schibboleth'" and the authorial calling out "ich, Celan" are shibboleth-apostrophes suspended between multiple pronunciations and breathless cuts, poly(a)phonic, apopneumatic.

# 7
# S(c)hibboleth
*Babel*

Does *Schibboleth* translate as *shibboleth*? "Nur in der Muttersprache kann man die eigene Wahrheit aussagen, in der Fremdsprache lügt der Dichter": only in the mother tongue can one declare one's own truth, Celan reportedly said, when reproached for writing in the language of the murderers of his parents; "in a foreign tongue the poet lies."[1] Celan has come to exemplify, for Western European literature, a predicament that has itself become exemplary of damaged life. For the survivor, to "declare one's own truth" is to speak the unspeakable; and for the poet as survivor, language, and only language, remains. For convenience, and only for now, call that language German, though Celan crucially never does so in the Bremen prize acceptance speech, but speaks rather of "die Sprache" as the one thing [*dies eine*] that remains unlost [*unverloren*] amid all losses [*Verluste*]:

> Yes, language [*die Sprache*], despite everything,
> remained un-lost. But it had to go through [*hindurch-
> gehen*] its own lack of answers, go through [*hindurch-*

*gehen*] terrifying silence, go through the thousand
darknesses of death-bringing speech [*hindurchgehen
durch die tausend Finsternisse todbringender Rede*]. It
went through and gave no words for what was happening; but it went through this happening. Went through
and could resurface, "enriched" by it all [*Sie ging
hindurch und gab keine Worte her für das, was geschah;
aber sie ging durch dieses Geschehen. Ging hindurch
und durfte wieder zutage treten, "angereichert" von all
dem*].[2]

At once a chant and a stutter, the reiterated *hindurchgehen—
hindurchgehen—hindurchgehen—ginghindurch—gingdurch—
ging hindurch* enacts the traumatic passage it describes: an
aporetic going-through that carves the scare quotes, as the apt
English phrase has it, around "enriched," "angereichert."[3]
Language has been "enriched" precisely insofar as it "gave
no words" for the happening, *das Geschehen*: insofar as it
gave no words for the lack of answers, the terrifying silence,
and the darknesses of death-bringing speech through which
it went. Language is shibboleth because it went through. It
went through the disappearance of the mother and the loss
of the world: it was the one thing, *dies eine*, that was un-lost,
*unverloren*; it remained as *un-*. It was "enriched" by being
scored and harrowed by its *un-*, by a muteness that must
speak. If there is a mother tongue, it will be the black milk
that forces its way through "Todesfüge"; if there is poetry, it
will be written in the language of stone.[4] The language of
the poem will then no longer best be called "German" or
any other name susceptible of ethnic or national derivation.
In an evocative phrase, Thomas Schestag suggests, apropos
of various texts by Celan, that "it is not so much that the
poem is written *in* a language, *in* several languages, as that
language, languages, immigrate *into* the poem."[5] The poem

is underway: its language(s) is/are migratory, immigrating in from elsewhere.

Celan endured the "monolingualism of the other" unsparingly. Derrida was of course differently situated in a different linguistic-cultural-historical matrix (as he puts it: a French-Algerian-Jew "thrown into absolute translation, a translation without a pole of reference, without an originary language, and without a source language [*langue de départ*]").[6] But he and Celan intersected at a meridian point at which the word *Schibboleth* could slide into focus. As the first markedly Hebraic word to feature prominently in a poem of Celan's,[7] *Schibboleth* may fairly be taken, in one sense, as a password and test and signal (indeed, for the anti-Semite, a supplemental *no pasarán*), beamed out to a suspect readership in Adenauer's Germany. Yet we have seen that Celan's poems transform *Schibboleth* into an affirmation beyond testing, and into the sign of language in its citability and plurality. And we have also seen that Celan's texts (and Derrida's after them) release a potential already at work in this strange word, as readers of the Bible inherit it. *S(c)hibboleth* is the mark that identifies the (m)other-tongue-speaker, yet it is also the mark of the other "within," "without," and "as" the mother tongue — any so-called mother tongue. For no language can fully claim this word ("if it is one"). As soon as *shibboleth* begins migrating and adapting across languages, it no longer properly belongs even to biblical Hebrew, for only past the border of the biblical text does it become the word for test-word (the word that means itself as a word that, *as* test-word, as we saw, loses not just its meaning but even in a sense its form, and is no longer securely a word). In German one might want to call it an exemplary *Fremdwort*: a foreign word that has undergone a degree of linguistic integration, and that therefore neither belongs simply to a different language (like, say, the phrase *no pasarán*, or *Peuple/de*

*Paris*), nor to the naturalized body-republic of the *Muttersprache* (like, say, *Februar*, a Latin immigrant long ago granted citizenship). Yet this particular *Fremdwort* has a supplemental touch of foreignness. Writing his 1954 letter to Isac Chiva—another Romanian-Jewish Holocaust survivor who settled in France—in which he enclosed his still unpublished poem, Celan felt the urge to insert a macaronic parenthesis about the word *Schibboleth*: "(c'est un mot d'origine hébreue [*sic*] qui se trouve dans l'Ancien Testament, en allemand cela veut dire à peu près *Erkennungszeichen*)"; "(it is a word of Hebrew origin found in the Old Testament, in German it means more or less *Erkennungszeichen* [sign of recognition])" (Wiedemann, 728). In German as in other languages (yet of course above all in German), the no-longer-simply-Hebrew word *Schibboleth* is uncertainly assimilated.[8] "*Fremdwörter* are the Jews of language," Adorno comments in *Minima Moralia*.[9] Adorno famously sought to read in the *Fremdwort* a token of redemption. In his early essay, "On the Use of Foreign Words," *Fremdwörter* take a foreign stance toward language itself: "sie stehen fremd zur Sprache."[10] The *Fremdwort* is "the dead-tired messenger from the future kingdom of language" (11:644/290); it registers "a hidden language that is unknown in the positive sense, a language that overtakes, overshadows, and transfigures the existing one, as though it were getting ready to be transformed into the language of the future. . . . The power of an unknown, genuine language that is not open to any calculus, a language that arises only in pieces and out of the disintegration of the existing one" (11:645–646/291). Adorno returned to this theme a quarter century later in "Words from Abroad" (1959), proposing that *Fremdwörter* "could preserve something of the utopia of language, of a language without earth [*einer Sprache ohne Erde*], without subjection to the spell of historical existence. . . . Hopelessly, like death's heads, they await their awakening in a better order of things."[11] To be without soil, *ohne Erde*, would be to transcend the *nomos* of the earth as division and bordering—the locus where *shibboleth* unfolds as sovereign violence. Celan is at once more cautious and more radical than Adorno: in the poems we have examined, *shibboleth* lays bare an opening and a motion that precedes, enables, and ruins *nomos* understood in the primordial sense that Schmitt famously sought to recover ("the first measure of subsequent measures, the first land appropriation").[12] Yet we doubtless catch an echo here of a conversation that never quite took place—one of several making up the Celan-Adorno dossier. *Im Herzmund / erwachtes Schibboleth*.

*Shibboleth*, the always-already-foreign-ish word that marks and ruins borders among what are called languages, is the lesson of Babel: a story that holds more in reserve on this point for us than standard interpretations of it suggest. Let us return to the Bible. "And the whole earth was of one language, and one speech"; and the sons of Shem propose to make a city, a tower, and a name:

> And they said to one another, Go to, let us make brick, and burn them thoroughly. And they had brick for stone, and slime had they for mortar. And they said, Go to, let us build a city and a tower, whose top may reach unto heaven; and let us make a name, lest we be scattered abroad upon the face of the whole earth. And the Lord came down to see the city and the tower, which the children of men builded. And the Lord said, Behold, the people is one, and they have all one language; and this they begin to do; and now nothing will be restrained from them, which they have imagined to do. Go to, let us go down, and there confound their language, that they may not under-

stand one another's speech. So the Lord scattered
them abroad from thence upon the face of all the
earth; and they left off to build the city. Therefore is
the name of it called Babel; because the Lord did
there confound [בלל, *balal*] the language of all the
earth: and from thence did the Lord scatter them
abroad upon the face of all the earth. (Genesis 11:1–9)

The verb that the King James translators translate as "confound," *balal*, literally means "mix": "It is a little-used verb employed elsewhere in the Bible only for mixing the ingredients fine flour and oil to make offertory cakes or bread."[13] The "unusual choice," as Theodore Hiebert calls it, of *balal* to describe Yahweh's action (instead of, say, *nifal*, divide, as in the previous chapter, Genesis 10:5, where linguistic division appears already to have occurred: "By these were the isles of the Gentiles divided in their lands; every one after his tongue") grants the story folk-etymological and satiric punch, thanks to the phonetic similarity between this Hebrew word and the name Babel (a name that, as might be expected, has a more dignified meaning in Babylonian: "gate of the gods"). It also produces a chord of anagrammatic echoes: "let us mix" [נבלה, *nblh*] is an anagram of "let us make bricks" [נלבה, *nlbh*] and of "let us build" [נבנה, *nbnh*]. Yahweh's act resonates in the text's scrambling of signifiers. The mixing is already in (the story of) the speech act that calls for baking and building, the arche-technic. (Bruegel proposes just this in his famous *Tower of Babel*, a painting from 1563 that shows us human figures "communicating" and "working"—but only insofar as Yahweh has always already descended into language-as-techne itself, causing the Tower to pile up as architectonic confusion [Figure 1].)[14] For although the story plots an equation—language plus God (as confusion) equals languages (as confusion)—the

Figure 1. Pieter Bruegel the Elder, *The Tower of Babel*, 1563, panel, Kunsthistorisches Museum, Vienna.

most far-reaching implication of the verb "mix" is that Yahweh adds nothing to language except a force that cannot be said to be properly "outside" language, except insofar as language is already outside of itself. Yahweh's hands (so to speak) are "in" language (so to speak) as he mixes language with language, kneads language into languages, makes language into what it already is, if it is to be mixable at all: plural, divided, on the move.[15] "Babel within a single language," Derrida writes; it has been there all along, *nachträglich*, the shibboleth mix.[16] The mixing is itself mixed, ahead of and behind its narrative mooring: in other words—stirred and baked differently—a certain "(un)translat*ability*" will be at work in and as language even as Yahweh stirs up the confusion that makes translation at once necessary and impossible. The story of Babel offers narrative counterpoint to Benjamin's dense proposition that "the impart*able* is immediately language itself" ("dieses Mitteil*bare* ist unmittelbar die Sprache selbst"). Language im-parts and parts in and from itself, and *shibboleth* names at once the untranslatable—the reserve of language that the poem "is"—and the trans-latio, the carrying across, that the poem also cherishes and for which it calls.[17]

Babel generates the fantasy of a pure translation: the erasure of *shibboleth*, which is also to say the erasure of literature and for that matter of language itself, along with every possibility of a *Fremdwort* or a *Hindurchgehen*, a passing-through and living-on. That fantasy of language purified to zero is woven into the theological fabric of commodity exchange, capitalism, and modern technics. As technology penetrates ever further into social life, computer translation programs and prosthetic devices (for instance, at the time of this writing, earpieces that Google has been developing to provide real-time translation) begin to approach the magical machines of which science fiction has long dreamed. In William Gibson's cyberpunk novels from the 1980s, characters insert "microsofts" into their skulls to acquire specialized bodies of knowledge, including languages: "The structure of Spanish settled through him, like a tower of glass, invisible gates hinged on present and future, conditional, preterite perfect."[18] That tower of glass would be Babel techno-retrofitted and purified, its fired bricks burned to transparency. To be sure, the software only provides "a limited fluency in Spanish" (3). Will the next release take another step toward allowing a prosthetically enhanced subject perfect mastery over *shin* and *sin* and any other mark that makes a difference—every shade of accent, every nuance of a targeted dialect? Not in Gibson's text, at least: a writer subtle enough to evoke Babel in the very image of its overcoming ("like a tower of glass") knows that the divine promise of pure translation is also the promise of confusion.[19]

That lesson is readable in the story of Pentecost, the great restitutive supplement to Babel that announces the global reach of a proselytizing religion committed to media and mediatization, and the dissemination of its good news:

> And when the day of Pentecost was fully come, they were all with one accord in one place. And suddenly there came a sound (*êchos*) from heaven as of a rushing mighty wind, and it filled all the house where they were sitting. And there appeared unto them cloven tongues like as of fire (*diamerizomenai glôssai hôsei puros*), and it sat upon each of them. And they were all filled with the Holy Ghost (*Pneumatos Hagiou*), and began to speak with other tongues (*êrxanto lalein heterais glôssais*), as the Spirit gave them utterance. And there were dwelling at Jerusalem Jews, devout men, out of every nation under heaven. Now when this was noised abroad (this voice or sound having arisen: *genomenês de tês phônês tautes*), the multitude came together (*sunêlthen to plêthos*), and were confounded (*sunechuthê*), because that every man (each one: *heis hekastos*) heard them speak in his own language (*dialektô*). And they were all amazed and marvelled (*ethaumazon*), saying one to another, Behold, are not all these which speak Galileans? And how hear we every man in our own tongue (*dialektô*), wherein we were born (*egennêthêmen*)? Parthians, and Medes, and Elamites, and the dwellers in Mesopotamia, and in Judaea, and Cappadocia, in Pontus, and Asia, Phrygia, and Pamphylia, in Egypt, and in the parts of Libya about Cyrene, and strangers of Rome, Jews and proselytes, Cretes and Arabians, we do hear them speak in our tongues (*glôssais*) the wonderful work of

God. And they were all amazed, and were in doubt, saying one to another, What meaneth this? Others mocking said, These men are full of new wine. (Acts 2:1–13)

In response to that closing bit of earthiness, the apostle Peter, who may or may not have a sense of humor but who is now divinely inspired in all matters communicational and can deliver a snappy line with a straight face, points out that it is still early morning (2:14–15). There is indeed a comic wildness to this scene. The crowd is hyperbolically diverse; it is the multitude of the world; and every single person making up that multitude is stunned and confounded, at once isolated and brought together with others in amazement. The amazement one feels, standing in this crowd, is partly that of hearing Galileans (a population known for having a strong regional accent) suddenly speaking one's own native tongue with (let us presume) "native" proficiency—that is amazing, to be sure; but even more amazing is one's simultaneous awareness that everyone *else* is hearing the same speech acts in *their* various native tongues: "how hear we every man in our own tongue, wherein we were born?" Let us give the miracle its full power: each one hears the speech acts of the apostles in the language, dialect, and idiom of his nativity; down to the tiniest linguistic difference marking out the smallest region, town, tribe, family; down to the most private nuance, the most secret sign. And yet each hearer also knows that it is also not so—knows that others are hearing something else; hearing, down to the last shade of expression, *their* languages. Pentecostal speech at once passes and fails the shibboleth-test at every moment and at every point. Pentecostal speech is simultaneously that of the mother as language, the mother tongue ("wherein we were born"), and that of an other foreign enough to be every other in the world.

Each one hears the mother tongue and hears babel. No one is fooled; everyone is confused.

Addressed to each and every monolingual other, Pentecostal language is neither one nor many, nor a synthesis of the one and the many. The mother tongue is beside itself. This is why the Holy Spirit appears as "dividing (*diamerizomenai*) tongues as of fire." Or rather: it appears as a sound (*êchos*) from heaven that becomes dividing tongues, then passes through the mouths of the disciples, and then becomes a sound or voice or sound-of-voice (*phônê*, in the genitive absolute construction *genomenês de tês phônês tautes*) that at once brings together and fragments the multitude (*plêthos*), assembling it only to scatter it into linguistic singularities.[20] At once singular and split and uncountably plural—both more and less than *logos*, overflowing the linguistic communion of the polis[21]—this dividing sound-voice-tongues is at once language and "language," language and its specter, language and languages, language im-parting. The miracle cure, the pharmakon for Babel, is another babel. (Like all miracles, the Pentecostal polylogue is a punctual wonder; it disappears over the narrative horizon like a healed leper, and we hear no more about apostles possessed of polyglot powers. What we get instead are occasional references to the Holy Ghost manifesting itself as "speaking in tongues": an inversion of Pentecostal speech insofar as few if any mortal auditors can understand glossolalia, at least according to Paul: "For he that speaketh in an unknown tongue speaketh not unto men, but unto God; for no man understandeth him" [1 Cor 14:2].)[22] Coming together (*sunêlthen*), the multitude is confused (*sunechuthê*)—and if *sunechuthê* and *sunêlthen* become hard to tell apart here, it becomes that much less surprising to hear (as we add a philological voice to this murmur) that the verb used for confusion (*suncheô*: to pour together, confound, confuse) is the verb used in the Septuagint to translate *balal* (with Babel renamed "Sunchusis" so as to translate the antonomasia: "Therefore he named it Babel [*Sunchusis*], for there Yahweh mixed [*sunecheen*] the language of all the earth").

The poem may be said to aspire to Pentecostal speech. Yet poetic language is non-evangelical; its worldiness and politicality—even, one can say, its mediality, its broadcasting— does not consist in the delivery of news, good or bad, but in finding a way, an aporetic way, in language(s), for its address. To find a way is to yield an opening and reserve a secret and perform a breath-turn as unpronounceable as a line break, and as pentecostally open as the quasi-silent translation, from, say, "German" *Schibboleth* to "English" *shibboleth*, the difference, in writing, of a capital letter and a *c*. Reading Celan, Derrida found a word for that finding of a way, and we have retraced that gesture here: "in a language, in the poetic writing of a language, there is nothing but *shibboleth*" (33). The word *shibboleth* itself, as noted at the beginning of this study, is not found very often anywhere: not very often in Derrida, except in the text we have examined; even less frequently in Celan, who uses the word only in the two poems we have engaged. Yet like circumcision, which, as we saw, Derrida assimilates to shibboleth, and which appears as the word *Beschneidung* only once in Celan, yet "as the *tropic* of circumcision disposes cuts, caesuras, ciphered alliances and wounded rings throughout the text" (54)—like circumcision, shibboleth scatters: scatters in and as an incalculable dissemination of cuts and ciphers, encryptions and crossings. An extended study of shibboleth in Celan would extend beyond any extendedness of study, beyond the finite act of any reading, even a reading extended ad infinitum. For even after exhaustively cataloguing tropes and motifs (starting, perhaps, with the only poem of Celan's with an English-language title, "Give the Word" in *Atemwende* [the citation is from *King Lear*, 4:6: *Lear*: Give the word. *Edgar*: Sweet marjoram. *Lear*: Pass]); even after rolling through the corpus, drawing boundaries and then violating them in a spiral of trying to keep up with proliferating figures of boundaries, passages, passings-through, passovers, dates, marks, wounds, stutters, cries; even after parsing every nonsemantic difference-making difference in every line, phrase and turn signed by Celan—even then, at the far end of that bad infinity, every poem would still withdraw, still guard its secret and remain open: open to reading, to withdrawal, to misuse, to disappearance, to absolute loss. For no holy spirit sustains it; the poem speaks of, to, and from the dead and it is consigned to death. ("Poetry, ladies and gentlemen—: this endless speaking of sheer mortality and finitude!")[23] Although, as noted earlier, Derrida (who usually tried to keep leverage terms contextually situated) invoked the word *shibboleth* infrequently after his 1986 text on Celan, he was drawn to it while formulating a relation between death and the secret in *Aporias* (1993):

> Death is always the name of a secret, since it signs the irreplaceable singularity. It puts forth the public name, the common name of a secret, the common name of the proper name without name. It is therefore always a shibboleth, for the manifest name of a secret is from the beginning a private name, so that language about death is nothing but the long history of a secret society, neither public nor private, semi-private, semi-public, on the border between the two; thus, also a sort of hidden religion of the awaiting (oneself as well as each other), with its ceremonies, cults, liturgy. . . . [24]

In this context, it is worth noting that early drafts of the poem that became "Schibboleth" did not feature the word *Schib-*

*boleth*, toward which the poem, like a casting animal, had to sense its way. When the word eventually made its appearance, it did so twice in succession, in haunting lines that Celan later for the most part excised. Here *Schibboleth* is the object of reflexive apostrophe, called to call itself out and make itself known, as the *Herz* will be in the final version:

> Schibboleth
> Gib dich zu erkennen:
> Rufe das Schibboleth,
> darin sich die Toten begegnen[25]

> Shibboleth
> Make yourself known:
> Call the shibboleth,
> in it the dead meet each other

The word responds to the call, to its own call, and appears—though as we know, nothing is less certain than that the word *Schibboleth* names or performs the shibboleth. *Schibboleth* is always also the name of a secret, an irreducibly uncertain name for "language about death." As he revised, Celan pushed the address to *Schibboleth* back into the fabric of the poem that he was now titling "Schibboleth," and he virtualized the prepositional qualification "darin sich die Toten begegnen" into a possible resonance of the *Stimmen*, the voices, of Estremadura. The dead were removed and buried elsewhere and allowed to return as ghosts. But one way (and it is perhaps too flatly assertive a way, which is perhaps why the line had to leave the poem)—one way to name the promise of shibboleth as poetic language is to say that in its secret the dead encounter each other.

## 8
## *Shibboleth*
Salcedo

That impossible encounter haunts the art of the Colombian artist Doris Salcedo, whose installation *Shibboleth* at the Tate Modern in 2007 brought renewed attention (although, I shall be suggesting, not enough or the right kind of attention) to this strange word. Commissioned as an installation in the Unilever series for the Tate's vast Turbine Hall, *Shibboleth* was a zigzagging crack in the museum floor that ran the entire 167-meter length of the hall (Figure 2a), varying in width from a thin fissure to a chasm several inches across, with embedded steel mesh fence visible where the crack was wide enough to expose its rough concrete sides (Figure 2b). The installation ran from October 9, 2007, to April 6, 2008, at which point the crack was filled in, leaving a scar on the floor of the gallery. The work received considerable media attention, partly because it so powerfully reimagined (but did not simply refuse) the monumentalizing demand of the venue; partly because a tiny number of museumgoers injured themselves stumbling over it; and partly because the work could be received—to the artist's understandable frustration—

Figure 2a and 2b (detail). Doris Salcedo, *Shibboleth*, 2007. Concrete and steel, length: 167 m (548 ft). Installation view at Turbine Hall, Tate Modern, London, 2007. © the artist. Courtesy Alexander and Bonin Gallery (New York) and White Cube.

as a bravura feat of engineering: one that, as an "abyss" that "tore the Tate in two," delivered existential excitement while inspiring speculation as to how it had been made, and whether or not the museum's floor had in fact been riven asunder.[1] The answer to that last question is of course no, architectonically speaking. In coming into being, *Shibboleth* had to replay the institutional complicity that enables and burdens all art, and it cracked the Turbine Hall floor only in a mediated and to some extent trompe-l'oeil way that, unlike actual earthquake damage or the fissure afflicting Poe's doomed House of Usher, did not, from an engineering perspective, "compromise the building's structural integrity."[2] Yet this sculpture-installation was also never simply the sum of its own artifice. If it has continued to overstay its visa, lingering on underfoot to inflect other installations in the Turbine

Hall, its persistence past itself as a mark in the museum floor functions as the signature of an afterlife that in fact began as soon as the installation began, via image, video recording, and narrative description. The scar or residue lives on as a reminder of the installation's finitude—its datedness—and therefore also of the work's irreducibility to presence and self-presence.

In this context, the work's title, which has received only cursory mention even in strong and informed writing on this artwork, demands the kind of consideration that the present study has enabled.[3] Salcedo's *Shibboleth* is also a name, a word and an unword; and her title quite probably refers intentionally to Celan and to Derrida on Celan (and, of course, to other texts, dates, cuts, and occasions that form part of the artwork's secret), in addition to the story in Judges. Salcedo used English translations of phrases from poems by Celan as subtitles of her *Unland* series in the 1990s, and she selected extracts from *The Meridian* and from four poems by Celan, along with some paragraphs from Emmanuel Levinas's *Otherwise Than Being*, as her "Artist's Choice" texts for a volume in her honor in 2000; in more recent interviews and statements she has continued to refer her thinking to Celan, and to Derrida, Levinas, and other major figures in the Continental tradition.[4] *Shibboleth* may very well, therefore, be citing and translating Celan's "Schibboleth" and Derrida's *Schibboleth*. That possibility is of course uninsurable, not least because *shibboleth* is always already a citation and a translation and a secret; but such undecidability is as much a spur as a hinderance to reading.

In the context of contemporary art production and consumption, an artwork can never be entirely quarantined from its title (even if that title is *Untitled*, let alone *Shibboleth*), any more than it can from the artist's signature (these things can of course go missing, or never exist in the first place, but that involves other contexts). Yet titles, it seems, slip easily out of view, particularly if the work has the visual, conceptual, and, in an extended sense, textual power that *Shibboleth* does. If one imagines this work untitled (as the secondary literature sometimes seems to do), one imagines it would still evoke the violence of border control and indeed—in tension with the installation's presentation as a stationary crevice in the floor—the mobility of modern border technology. The gleaming suture-like stitches of steel mesh in the sides of the crack incorporate into the work one of the major technical innovations—the wire fence—that made the modern concentration camp and refugee camp possible, along with much zoning of space throughout contemporary life. As Rebecca Comay remarks, wire fencing is "scary stuff" that "can be used variously for purposes of fortification, incarceration, protection, exclusion, and segregation," and is "particularly useful for erecting temporary and not-so-temporary structures—camps, construction sites, military compounds, detention centres, playgrounds, parking lots, prisons—and for staking out the fluctuating but inviolable borders of private property and state" (51). The jagged, branching crack in the exhibition floor, flecked with wire like a wound with shrapnel, spurs politico-aesthetic allegories. We can imagine that an untitled *Shibboleth* (though the title will no doubt also already be seeping through our barrier, contaminating our pseudo-phenomenological experiment) would easily be interpreted as addressing the never-ending global refugee crisis, or more broadly, the policing of populations, groups and individuals in an ever more mobile and unequal postcolonial and neoliberal global order. The monumental scale of the work permits yet grander generalizations. Writing in a broadly Hegelian vein, Mieke Bal claims that *Shibboleth* "signifies nothing, and at the same time, because of that negativity, everything. . . . The incised or 'inscripted' negative space opens up an abyss of unlimited meaning" (236). And since *Shibboleth* is (or was—but such discussions inevitably drift into the present tense) an artwork fissuring the floor of the biggest exhibition hall of one of the planet's most famous museums, it reads as a commentary on art, the art world, and museums. The wound would be *of* the museum, subjective and objective genitive. The artwork, figuratively wounding the museum, figures the wounding of colonized cultures by the museal-aesthetic culture of (post)colonial powers. Thus Claudette Lauzon suggests that Salcedo's work "connect[s] the building to a colonial history of exclusion and exploitation that underpins the modernism celebrated within [it]," offering a critique not just of the old-fashioned museum but also of the "privileged nomadism" of the postmodern art world (138–139). And with such reflections comes the familiar, stubborn problematic of testamentary art and indeed, if one follows Adorno, of all art. In Comay's eloquent summary: "The challenges have been well-rehearsed: how to commemorate an event which both demands and refuses commemoration; where all available cultural forms threaten to trivialise, sentimentalise, mystify, embellish, instrumentalise, or otherwise betray the memory of the dead; and where every attempt to acknowledge injury seems to compound the injury" (42). Salcedo's work bears witness to the mind-numbing scale of suffering in Colombia, and often commemorates a particular atrocity suffered there; she is known for the extent of her research into a case, and also for the rigor with which she excludes explanations and references from the finished work. Salcedo's work commemorates but does not report. It accepts the risk of abstraction and aestheticization, of a further loss and effacement of the injury it mourns.[5] It forwards an impossible responsibility, which the work seeks to make not so much visible or palpable as legible. In some cases, as noted earlier, Salcedo has used titles and subtitles to force this point, as when, in the *Unland* series, she summons bits of poems by Celan to become part of works that refuse to be intuited aesthetically, and demand instead to be read.

Only the last of these reflections (and it is, to be sure, a decisive one) appears to require much consideration of the title *Shibboleth*, though taking this title into account clearly at the very least enriches and amplifies the political and ethical allegories that critics (including Salcedo herself) have proposed.[6] The artwork pronounces its word that much more clearly, speaking to us of a meshwork of testing and sorting, control and sequestration, where linguistic and semiotic nuances can play as decisive a role as wire fencing and reinforced concrete. The varying width of the crack evokes that much more sharply the inequalities sustained by wide gaps and hairline differences, reminding us that micro- as well as macro-mechanisms of control enable the mass production of death, whether as punctual murder or as slow killing. We become, perhaps, a little more alert to the complex winnowing mechanisms at work even (or especially) in massively popular museum spaces; to the global reach of the financial and cultural filtering systems that enable monumental displays. Yet at the same time the title, at once part of and at the edge of the work, opens another fissure. Like the artist's implied signature and like the images and narratives of the buried installation, the title persists and circulates, naming the ensemble of those images and narratives (including the scar that is their funerary mark) and functioning in all the legal, archival, and liminal ways that titles do.[7] But the title is a name that also functions as a meaning: it presents itself as the ground of a figure (which is how we take it when we say that it enriches and amplifies the allegories that the work generates). Yet the ground is a chasm, for the title is also a citation and a citational performative: a repetition (one that would be "*in a peculiar way* hollow or void," in J. L. Austin's famous phrase: there would be a fissure in the floor of this performative) of the legendary biblical test-word speech act, which itself, as we have seen, splits and doubles into unreliable echoes of an originary splitting and echoing.[8] Sovereign or pseudo-sovereign acts of terrible violence occur over and in denegation of that abyss; yet a different speech act also finds its chance there, a call or prayer or apostrophe that echoes down the chain of titles we have cited here, by Salcedo, Derrida, Celan. Reading Salcedo with Celan, we find ourselves returned to the excised lines from "Schibboleth" that we cited earlier: "Rufe das Schibboleth/darin sich die Toten begegnen."[9] This removed and buried call to call for the shibboleth in which the dead meet one another does not yield to mysticism. This apostrophe, which is a breath-turn and a cut, would not animate the dead. The dead have spectral life to give; they haunt the living ceaselessly; but here another call, a muted and breathless one, is being inscribed. In this awaited shibboleth the dead would not speak but meet, not with the living but with each other. Meeting, *begegnen*, involves an irreducible element of chance, and carries the uncertain promise of a touch. Irreparable losses would gather, *in eins*, in this secret beyond pronunciation, and the poetic I would be mindful of its dates in exposing itself to an act of mourning that concerns only the dead.

# Acknowledgments

This short book has ended up being mainly about Paul Celan—its subtitle is a tricolon crescens. The project had its origin, however, in a brief consideration of the shibboleth episode in Judges, as part of a paper focused on different texts than the ones examined here, written for a colloquium in honor of Samuel Weber that took place at the Château de la Bretesche in Missillac, France, in the summer of 2010. Some years later, an invitation from Tim Bewes and Adi Ophir to offer a lecture in the "Political Concepts" series at Brown University provided the impetus to think more about the story in Judges and the word and concept *shibboleth*, and the readings then developed by way of talks given for literature and humanities departments at Brown University, CUNY Graduate Center, Katholieke Universiteit Leuven, the University of Budapest, UC Berkeley, UC Riverside, and the University of Oregon. Fragments of this project were also presented as papers at ACLA conferences in Utrecht and Los Angeles. I have profited from the rich discussions that ensued on each occasion; some specific debts are recorded in endnotes. As I began to work seriously with the biblical text, I received help from Saul Olyan, Adi Ophir, and Tammi Schneider. It cannot be stressed too strongly that any philological errors in those sections of the text are my doing, not theirs. The book as a whole has been enriched by specific conversations with dear friends in the German Department at Brown: Susan Bernstein, Kristina Mendicino, Gerhard Richter, Thomas Schestag, and Zachary Sng. A course co-taught with Ourida Mostefai gave me an opportunity to discuss aspects of the project in a seminar format. Two exceptionally keen-eyed anonymous reader's reports helped me clarify and develop portions of the argument. The project was supported by travel grants and humanities research funds at Brown. I am grateful to the Tate Modern, to Alexander and Bonin Gallery (New York) and White Cube, and to Doris Salcedo for allowing me to reproduce images of Salcedo's *Shibboleth* (2007). Thanks to Tom Lay and the editorial and production team at Fordham University Press, and Lit Z series editors Sara Guyer and Brian McGrath. Thanks, finally and above all, to Molly Ierulli, the best philologist I know.

# Notes

## 1. Shibbloleth: Inheritance

1. Walter Benjamin, "Über einige Motive bei Baudelaire," in *Gesammelte Schriften*, ed. Rolf Tiedemann and Hermann Schweppenhäuser (Frankfurt am Main: Suhrkamp, 1974), 1.2, 647n; "On Some Motifs in Baudelaire," in *Selected Writings*, ed. Howard Eiland and Michael Jennings (Cambridge, MA: Harvard University Press, 2003), 4:354n77. Benjamin quotes from Karl Kraus, *Pro domo et mundo* (Munich: Albert Langen, 1912), 164.

2. A masculine version, *shibbelim*, meaning ears of grain, occurs multiple times in the story of Joseph's interpretation of Pharaoh's dream (Genesis 41:5–27) and three times in two other contexts (Ruth 2:2; Isaiah 17:5, twice). See Ludwig Koehler and Walter Baumgartner, *The Hebrew and Aramaic Lexicon of the Old Testament* (Leiden: Brill, 1999), 1394. I have also profited from the Abarim online *Biblical Dictionary* and the interlinear text provided by BibleHub.com.

3. Unless otherwise noted, quotations from the Hebrew Bible are taken from *The English Bible King James Version, I: The Old Testament*, ed. Herbert Marks (New York: Norton, 2012), and are given by conventional chapter and verse: here, Judges 12:5–6. The

Vaticanus manuscript of the Septuagint gives the Greek word *stachus* (ear of corn) as the test-word without attempting to reproduce a mispronunciation ("Then they said to him, Say now *stachus*, and he did not rightly pronounce it so"); the Alexandrinus manuscript translates *shibboleth* as *sunthêma* (password). In the Vulgate, Jerome splits the differences and covers all the bases: he at once preserves a transliteration of *shibboleth*, explains its meaning, and invents a mispronunciation: "interrogabant eum/dic ergo sebboleth quod interpretatur spica/qui respondebat tebboleth/eadem littera spicam non valens" ("they asked him/say then sebboleth which means ear of grain/and he responded tebboleth/by means of that same letter not able to express ear of grain").

4. Grimm does not have an entry for *Schibboleth*. Littré has a relatively robust one, with a citation from Balzac and a recollection of the biblical story. The word does not appear at all in the Italian, Portuguese, and Spanish dictionaries I have consulted, though these and many other languages have Wikipedia entries for the term. It takes slightly different orthographic form in different languages: e.g., Spanish and Italian, like English, use an initial *sh-*; Dutch and Icelandic have *sjibbolet*; Portuguese spells the word *xibolete*; Hungarian, in which the letter *s* is pronounced "sh," spells it *sibolet* (with the Ephraimitic pronunciation written *szibolet*).

5. Fowler's *Modern English Usage* (Oxford: Clarendon Press, 1965). The most recent edition I have consulted, ed. R. W. Burchfield (1996), offers a tamer entry but sticks to the basic idea: "1) It is first and foremost 'the Hebrew word used by Jephthah . . .'" (here Burchfield quotes from the account of Judges 12:4–6 in the full OED entry, given in the following note). "From this, from the 17c. onward, it has been used for any word or sound which a person is unable to pronounce correctly: hence a word or sound used to detect foreigners, or persons from another district. 2) By extension, from about the same time, it has been used to mean 'a long-standing formula, idea, phrase, etc. held (esp. unreflectingly) by or associated with a group, party, class, etc.'; and, nowadays, also 'an entrenched (political) belief or dogma.' Since there are

numerous synonyms available to express these extended senses, the word is best left at present restricted to the uses defined in 1" (709–710).

6. See https://en.oxforddictionaries.com/definition/shibboleth (accessed August 27, 2018). The old-fashioned print version of the *Oxford English Dictionary* offers a detailed entry that stays closer to the European restriction of the term while respecting the wider usage that it acquired in English. Here is a somewhat abbreviated version of the entry, with examples omitted: "1. The Hebrew word used by Jephthah as a test-word to distinguish the fleeing Ephraimites (who could not pronounce the *sh*) from his own men the Gileadites; 2. A word or sound which a person is unable to pronounce correctly; a word used as a test for detecting foreigners, or persons from another district, by their pronunciation; b) a peculiarity of pronunciation or accent indicative of a person's origin; c) loosely: A custom, habit, mode of dress, or the like, which distinguishes a particular class or set of persons; 3. fig. a) A catchword or formula adopted by a party or sect, by which their adherents or followers may be discerned, or those not their followers may be excluded; b) The mode of speech distinctive of a profession, class, etc.; c) Hence a moral formula held tenaciously and unreflectingly, esp. a prohibitive one; a taboo." Meanings 2b and 3a go back to the seventeenth century; the rather broader 2c and 3b are first attested in the early nineteenth century; with 3c, the English language extends the meaning of *shibboleth* well beyond what other European languages allow.

7. Accessed August 5, 2017. In contrast, the Wikipedia entries for *shibboleth* in all other languages that I have sampled stick closely to the definition of test-word as featured in the biblical story.

8. As recorded above, the OED lists developments going back to the seventeenth century, though the early nineteenth century seems to have been an important moment for the career of *shibboleth* in English. Samuel Johnson does not have an entry for it in his *Dictionary* of 1786; but a revision of Johnson's *Dictionary* ("with numerous corrections, and with the addition of several

thousand words") by H. J. Todd in 1827 shows the word *shibboleth* already branching into a strong secondary meaning: "A word which was made a criterion, whereby the Gileadites distinguished the Ephraimites in their pronouncing of *s* for *sh*: hence, in a figurative sense, the criterion of a party."

9. The word *cliché*, like *stereotype*, derives from nineteenth-century mass-reproductive technology: it was printer's jargon, in France, for a stereotype block.

10. Alphonso Lingis, "Anger," in *On Jean-Luc Nancy: The Sense of Philosophy*, ed. Darren Sheppard, Simon Sparks, and Colin Thomas (New York: Routledge, 1997), 197–215. It is instructive to recall the statistics that Lingis offers in his passionate denunciation of social inequality: e.g., "In the United States in the 1980s there was a massive transfer of wealth; today 20 percent of the population enjoy 48% of the wealth" (203). Twenty years later, things are of course far worse. The richest 1 percent of the U.S. population holds 38 percent of wealth in the U.S., and the richest 1 percent of the world's population holds 50 percent of the world's wealth; of that 1 percent, according to the most recent Oxfam report at present writing, twenty-six individuals now hold as much wealth as the 3.8 billion people making up the poorer half of the world's population.

11. Emily Apter, *Against World Literature: On the Politics of Untranslatability* (New York: Verso, 2013), 112.

12. See https://www.shibboleth.net (accessed September 12, 2017).

13. For a vivid contemporary example, see Eyal Weizman, *Hollow Land: Israel's Architecture of Occupation* (London: Verso, 2007): "The linear border, a cartographic imaginary inherited from the military and political spatiality of the nation state, has splintered into a multitude of temporary, transportable, and deployable and removable border-synonyms—'separation walls,' 'barriers,' 'blockades,' 'closures,' 'road blocks,' 'checkpoints,' 'sterile areas,' 'special security zones,' 'closed military areas' and 'killing zones'—that shrink and expand the territory at will" (6). See Apter, *Against World Literature*, 112–114, for a discussion of

the "diffused" state that draws on Weizman's work, among that of others.

14. See Avital Ronell, *The Test Drive* (Urbana: University of Illinois Press, 2008).

15. John Milton, *Samson Agonistes* [1672], 289. In Judges 8, the men of Succoth and Penuel refuse to help Gideon pursue the fleeing Midianites. The story of Jephthah and the shibboleth, which we shall be examining, is Judges 11–12; Samson's story is told in Judges 13–16. The shibboleth/death rhyme will of course be found now and then elsewhere in English-language poetry, if one goes looking. It appears, e.g., in Andrew Marvell's "The Loyal Scot," a poem probably written about the same time as Milton's tragedy: "Nation is all but name as shibboleth/Where a mistaken accent causes death" (262–263). Dryden does not rhyme with the word, but he does have the Hind refer to the Test Acts as "a deadly Shibboleth" in his poetico-political allegory *The Hind and the Panther* (III, 1076). Byron also refuses the rhyme in *Don Juan*, but grants the word *shibboleth* pride of place in a typically canny joke: "Juan who did not understand a word/Of English, save their shibboleth 'God damn!'" (XI, 12:1–2). Of the less canonical works I have sampled, an otherwise forgettable sonnet by Hartley Coleridge is perhaps worth flagging here for having risked a triple rhyme on faith/shibboleth/death: see *Poems by Hartley Coleridge* (London: E. Moxon, 1851), 2:53. It may also be added here, as an irrelevant but pleasant curiosity, that Samuel Taylor Coleridge used the letter *shin* as code for SH, his beloved Sarah Hutchinson, in his notebooks (I thank Yohei Igarashi for alerting me to this), though he does not seem ever to have availed himself of the word *shibboleth*.

16. I am grateful to Ashley Champagne of Brown University's Rockefeller Library for giving me pointers on how to do sweeps with the remarkable HathiTrust.org database, to which I owe the Marvell and Byron references above, and some of my generalizations about German literature and philosophy below. Of course, one gets many hits for *shibboleth* (or, in the French and German spelling, *schibboleth*) when searching gigantic archives, but its appearances are proportionally rare. The word appears once in

Rabelais, once in a minor novel by Balzac, a couple of times in Scott, and so on; none of these or the dozens of other comparable instances that such searches turn up seem (at least to this reader) particularly memorable. At stake in the present study is a question of inheritance that cannot be assessed with quantitative technologies. On inheritance, see the work of Gerhard Richter, perhaps above all *Verwaiste Hinterlassenschaften: Formen gespentischen Erbens* (Berlin: Matthes & Seitz, 2016).

17. William Faulkner, *Absalom, Absalom!* (New York: Library of America, 1990), 115. The scene is anticipated and followed by two more appearances of the word *shibboleth*: Charles Bon calls marriage "a formula, a shibboleth meaningless as a child's game" (97); Rosa Coldfield returns to this word to capture her inability to summon up conventional gestures of propriety and self-defense when Thomas Sutpen puts his hand on her head and announces that he plans to marry her: *"yes, lost all the shibboleth erupting of cannot, will not, never will in one red instant's fierce obliteration"* (135).

18. But here are a few highlights: Rosa is "motionless in the action and attitude of running" (115–116) and in a "dream state where you run without moving" (117); her "I" is alternately and uncertainly that which is stopped and the body that is possibly not stopped; when Judith says "Clytie," Clytemnestra drops her hand, but Rosa is then once again halted-and-not-halted by Judith saying "Yes, Rosa?" There is a sense in which her body keeps moving past the borders of the scene, though Rosa also never reaches—in this scene—the closed door.

19. Nor anywhere in Schiller, nor in Kafka, though once, in a humorous vein, in Goethe: "Weiß und schwarz Brot ist eigentlich das Schibboleth, das Feldgeschrei, zwischen Deutschen und Franzosen" ("white and black bread is in fact the shibboleth, the battle-cry, between Germans and French"). *Campagne in Frankreich 1792*, in *Goethes Werke*, ed. Erich Trunz (Munich: C. H. Beck, 1981) 10:188–363, here 240.

20. Adorno's two uses of the word (across, as Gerhard Richter has reminded me, roughly 14,000 pages of published work—and of course the other writers being invoked here have oeuvres of

comparable magnitude) appear in *Negative Dialektik* (where the word serves to sharpen a polemic, à la Hegel and Marx: the "system character" of existential *Angst* was "yesterday still the shibboleth of academic philosophy"); and in the essay "George und Hofmannsthal. Zum Briefwechsel: 1891–1906" (where, intriguingly, Adorno writes *Schibboleth* where one might have expected him to use a word like *Fetisch*: "like a shibboleth, the object is held up to impending ruin while appeals are made to its beauty"). See Theodor W. Adorno, *Gesammelte Schriften*, ed. Rolf Tiedemann et al. (Frankfurt am Main: Suhrkamp, 1977), 6:34–35 (for *Negative Dialektik*) and 10.1:233 (for the George and Hofmannsthal essay); in English, *Negative Dialectics* trans. E. B. Ashton (New York: Continuum, 1973), 24; and *Prisms*, trans. Samuel and Shierry Weber (Cambridge, MA: MIT Press, 1967), 222.

21. "Allerdings Produktion, Produktion, auf stets erweiterter Stufenleiter, lautet das Schibboleth." Karl Marx, *Das Kapital*, vol. 1, in *Marx-Engels Werke* 23:622; Karl Marx and Friedrich Engels, *Collected Works* (New York: International Publishers, 1996), 35:591. Other instances in which Marx uses the word *Schibboleth* are of a similar sort. Hegel, also a master of the tart polemic tone, does something a little more interesting in the foreword to the third edition of the *Enzyklopädie*, insofar as he activates (though without reflective commentary) what we shall see to be the troubled intimacy between *shibboleth* and the name of God. He is targeting critics who wrap themselves in religious self-righteousness while launching ad hominem attacks: "the shibboleth of this absolute authority is the *name of the Lord Jesus Christ* and the *assurance* that the Lord dwells in the hearts of these judges." G. W. F. Hegel, *Enzyklopädie der philosophischen Wissenschaften I*, in *Werke*, ed. Eva Moldenhauer and Karl Markus Michel (Frankfurt am Main: Suhrkamp, 1986), 8:34; *The Encyclopaedia Logic: Part 1 of the Encyclopaedia of Philosophical Sciences*, trans. T. F. Geraets, W. A. Suchting, and H. S. Harris (Indianapolis: Hackett, 1991), 19 (Hegel's emphasis).

22. The passages may be found in the *Gesammelte Werke* (London: Imago, 1940–49) and the *Standard Edition*, ed. and trans. James Strachey (London: Hogarth Press, 1953–64) as

follows: *Drei Abhandlung zur Sexualtheorie* / *Three Essays on Sexuality*, GW 5:127–28n2 / SE 7:226n1; *Das Ich und das Es* / *The Ego and the Id*, GW 13:239 / SE 19:13; *Neue Folge der Vorlesungen zur Einführung in die Psychoanalyse* / *New Introductory Lectures on Psychoanalysis*, GW 15:6 / SE 22:7.

23. The remark about the unconscious speaking many dialects is to be found in *The Claims of Psychoanalysis to Scientific Interest* (1913), GW 8:405 / SE 13:176. A different book than the present one (and a very long and rigorous book at that) would be required to assess the play of words, signifiers, and shibboleth-effects in Freud's work, particularly in the wake of the Lacanian inheritance. The writings on dreams and parapraxes would no doubt be the first texts to take up (one thinks of the baroque rebus that Freud constructs in analyzing the name *Signorelli* at the beginning of *The Psychopathology of Everyday Life* [1901] [GW 4:6–10 / SE 6:2–5]), but an attention to words and portions of words as points of access and blockage runs through the Freudian corpus. As a fetishistic stand-in for proper analysis, we may recall Freud's dramatic opening example in his paper on "Fetishism" (1927): a young man's pathology involves a shine (*Glanz*) on noses that only he can see, and that Freud discovers to be the effect of an interlinguistic pun on the English *glance*: "The patient had been brought up in an English nursery. . . . The fetish . . . had to be understood in English, not German" (GW 14:311 / SE 21:152). The work of Nicolas Abraham and Maria Torok would merit special attention in this context: see, e.g., *The Wolf Man's Magic Word: A Cryptonomy*, trans. Nicholas Rand (Minneapolis: University of Minnesota Press, 2005); like the original French version of 1976, this translation includes Jacques Derrida's rich introductory essay, "Fors."

24. Edgar Allan Poe, "The Fall of the House of Usher," in *Edgar Allan Poe: Poetry and Tales* (New York: Library of America, 1984), 317–336, here 320. At the end of the story the narrator sees the "blood-red moon" shining "vividly through that once barely-discernible fissure, of which I have before spoken as extending from the roof of the building, in a zigzag direction, to the base.

While I gazed, this fissure rapidly widened . . . and the deep and dark tarn at my feet closed sullenly and silently over the fragments of the 'House of Usher'" (335–336).

25. This irreducibility to knowledge is what makes the test-word a more interesting object of analysis than the password; the latter exceeds the domain of voice, breath and logos but does so on a cybernetic register and remains within the zone of the calculable so long as its key is not lost (which is, to be sure, a permanent possibility). The test-word, as we shall see, crumbles out of the domain of the logos in a more complex and disruptive way.

26. Most directly, in "Signature Event Context" (1971) and its polemical after-rider "Limited Inc a b c . . ." (1977): both conveniently available with additional material in Jacques Derrida, *Limited Inc*, ed. Gerald Graff (Evanston, IL: Northwestern University Press, 1988). For a study of the logic of targeting broadly inspired by Derrida's thought, see Samuel Weber, *Targets of Opportunity: On the Militarization of Thinking* (New York: Fordham University Press, 2005).

27. Derrida's text will be cited from Jacques Derrida, *Sovereignties in Question: The Poetics of Paul Celan*, ed. Thomas Dutoit and Outi Pasanen (New York: Fordham University Press, 2005). This volume collects *Shibboleth: For Paul Celan* (1–64), several other texts by Derrida on Celan that will be identified as needed, and in an appendix, Celan's *The Meridian*. Citations from *Shibboleth* will be given parenthetically with, if necessary for clarification, the short title *Shibboleth* (italicized to recall this text's originally separate publication as a book). The original French text consulted is *Schibboleth: Pour Paul Celan* (Paris: Galilée, 1986).

28. Derrida consistently italicizes *shibboleth*. The present text will allow this word to float in and out of italics and quotation marks: italics indicate that the word itself is being emphasized; a nonmarked font indicates that the term has drifted toward conceptual status (often also acquiring a definite article: "the" shibboleth); quotation marks stress the instability of these distinctions and the wobbliness of this word *as* a word, about which more later.

## 2. שיבולת: Judges

1. The surviving men of Benjamin are also told to steal wives from another Hebraic community in Shiloh (21:16–24). The phrase "In those days there was no king in Israel" is repeated four times late in Judges (17:6; 18:1; 19:1; 21:25), characterizing this era as a period of anarchy prior to the establishment of the kingship. See Mieke Bal, *Death and Dissymmetry: The Politics of Coherence in the Book of Judges* (Chicago: University of Chicago Press, 1988), for an analysis of the intertribal and misogynistic violence in the text.

2. For an insightful feminist and structuralist discussion of Jephthah's sacrifice of his daughter, see Bal, *Death and Dissymmetry*, 109–113. For a study of the structure and major themes of Judges, see Tammi Schneider, *Judges* (Collegeville, MN: Liturgical Press, 2000). Human sacrifice is condemned by Israelite law (Leviticus 18:21, 20:2). I am not competent to offer an opinion as to whether the supposedly Canaanite practice of child sacrifice was practiced at times in ancient Israel; it does seem to form part of the constant temptation toward other gods to which the Israelites are subject (see the following note on 2 Kings 16:3 and 21:6). Human sacrifice is denounced in Micah 6:7, Jeremiah 3:24 and elsewhere, and Ezekiel 16:20–21 and 23:37–39. For a discussion of these passages, see E. John Hamlin, *Judges: At Risk in the Promised Land* (Edinburgh: Hansel Press, 1990), 118.

3. Child sacrifice, forbidden in Leviticus 18:21 and Deuteronomy 18:10, possibly numbers among the profanations of Ahaz, who "made his son pass through the fire" (2 Kings 16:3) and of Manasseh, who did the same (2 Kings 21:6), though the reference may be to a divinatory ritual. Jephthah's act, in contrast, forms the climax of a narrative elaboration, even as it is shrouded in the tautology of the deadly oath ("did with her according to his vow which he had vowed"). It makes for a grim counterpoint to the Abraham and Isaac story.

4. This philological summary relies on the following studies: E. A. Speiser, "The Shibboleth Incident (Judges 12:6)," in *Oriental*

*and Biblical Studies* (Philadelphia: University of Pennsylvania Press, 1967), 143–150; Gary A. Rendsburg, "More on Hebrew *sibbolet*," *Journal of Semitic Studies* 33 (1986): 255–258; P. Swiggers, "The Word *sibbolet* in Judg. XII.6," *Journal of Semitic Studies* 26 (1981): 205–207. The best guess seems to be that east of the Jordan, where the Gileadites were, an old-Canaanite *th* had been retained, which in the western regions had been overtaken by *s* and *sch*. Rendsburg, Speiser, and Swiggers all agree that the Gileadites were probably requesting a *t-* or *th*-sound; Swiggers thinks the Ephraimites would have responded with a *sh*, while Rendsburg and Speiser argue for *s*. Obviously the historical reconstruction of speech patterns is inherently speculative, and any number of subtle differences in pronunciation might lie behind the opposition of *shin* and *sin* (or the *samekh* that substitutes for *sin*).

5. Jack M. Sasson, *Judges 1–12: A New Translation with Introduction and Commentary*, The Anchor Yale Bible, vol. 6D (New Haven, CT: Yale University Press, 2014), 454.

6. Jack M. Sasson, "Jephthah: Chutzpah and Overreach in a Hebrew Judge," in *Literature as Politics: Politics as Literature: Essays on the Ancient Near East in Honor of Peter Machinist*, ed. David S. Vanderhooft and Abraham Winitzer (Winona Lake, IN: Eisenbrauns, 2013), 405–420, here 419. Mizpah is the town from which Jephthah presumably reigned—it is where he had his house in which his daughter lived prior to her sacrifice. Tov or Tob is where Jephthah lived in exile after being expelled by his brothers at the beginning of the story.

7. Willem F. Smelik, *The Targum of Judges* (Leiden: E. J. Brill, 1995), 556. This intriguing detail is from a marginal note found in a particular manuscript of the Targum; but the scattering of Jephthah's body, as Sasson notes, appears in rabbinical commentary. For discussion and documentation, see Smelik, *The Targum of Judges*, 555–556.

8. The status of the Gilead tribe is not clear in the Bible (ancient bits of text such as the Song of Deborah list Gilead as one of the tribes of Israel, while not mentioning others, including Manasseh), but the taunt of the Ephraimites accords

with a prominent line of genealogical inference. The land of
Gilead is divided up by Moses, who gives portions of it to
Reuben, Gad, and above all the half-tribe of Manasseh, which
is the tribe most strongly identified with the toponym (see
Numbers 32:40 and Deuteronomy 3:12–15). In the Book of Joshua,
as the Mosaic assignations are being confirmed and fine-tuned,
we learn of a "Gilead" (not the father of Jephthah) who is the son
of Machir, who is the firstborn of Manasseh (Joshua 17:1–3). If
the Gileadites do descend from Manasseh, the fraternity linking
Gileadites and Ephraimites is shadowed by Ephraim having
received his grandfather Jacob's blessing, displacing his older
brother Manasseh (Genesis 48:20). The favored younger son
motif, which returns to Cain and Abel, rolls back through the
patriarchs: Joseph gained precedence over ten older brothers;
Jacob stole Esau's birthright; Isaac took the place of Ishmael. It
may be added (just as a curiosity, since this has no obvious link
with the shibboleth episode) that the Ephraimites come in for
condemnation in Psalm 78:9ff: "The children of Ephraim, being
armed and carrying bows, turned back in the day of battle. / They
kept not the covenant of God, and refused to walk in his law; / And
forgot his works, and his wonders that he had shewed them."
Although the motives of the psalmist seem clear insofar as he is
giving precedence to Judah, the specific charge against the
Ephraimites remains a matter of philological speculation. See
F. A. Gosling, "Were the Ephraimites to Blame?" *Velus
Testamentum* 49, no. 4 (1999): 505–513, for a consideration of an
exegetical tradition that includes a fascinating gloss in the Targum
affirming that the sons of Ephraim, out of pride, left Egypt
without waiting for Moses, three years before the appointed
time (510).

### 3. S(h)ibboleth: Sovereign Violence and the Remainder

1. I thank Ortwin de Graef for alerting me to the case of the
Matins de Bruges (still famous in Flemish-speaking Belgium).
On the massacre in the Dominican Republic, see Arnaud Richard
and Renauld Govain, "Schibboleth, la langue comme arme de

détection massive: 1937, le massacre des Haïtiens," *Lengas: Revue de Sociolinguistique* 80 (2016), http://journals.openedition.org/lengas/1193 (accessed January 16, 2019). I thank Ourida Mostefai for alerting me to that article and Ian Sampson for informing me that the "Parsley Massacre" provides an anchor point for Caroline Bergvall's poem "Say: Parsley," in *Fig* (Cambridge: Salt, 2005), 58–59. The poem is also part of a multimedia installation, *Say Parsley*, developed with the composer Ciarán Maher, first mounted in November 2001 at the Spacex Gallery of the Exeter Maritime Museum and subsequently in other venues and contexts.

2. Johann Gottlieb Fichte, *Reden an die deutsche Nation* (Hamburg: Felix Meiner, Verlag, 1978), 207; *Addresses to the German Nation*, ed. and trans. Gregory Moore (Cambridge: Cambridge University Press, 2008), 166. For a careful exegesis of this moment in Fichte, see Etienne Balibar, "Fichte and the Internal Border," in *Masses, Classes, Ideas: Studies on Politics and Philosophy Before and After Marx*, trans. James Swenson (New York: Routledge, 1994), 61–84.

3. The irreducibility of borders to fixed geographic marks or barriers has been emphasized by scholars working in so-called border studies in recent years; see, e.g., Thomas Nail, *Theory of the Border* (New York: Oxford University Press, 2016). Nail usefully conceives of borders as hybrid circulation zones that are permeable, shifting, and contested. His loosely Deleuze-inspired idiom of "flow" and the interruption of flow, however, does not allow him to take account of the kind of phantasmatic excess that, as we shall see, an analysis of *shibboleth* has to attempt to think.

4. See Carl Schmitt, *The Concept of the Political*, trans. George Schwab (Chicago: University of Chicago Press, 2007).

5. Ferdinand de Saussure, *Cours de linguistique générale*, ed. Tullio de Mauro (Paris: Éditions Payot, 1972), 32.

6. Jacques Derrida, *Shibboleth: For Paul Celan*, in *Sovereignties in Question: The Poetics of Paul Celan*, ed. Thomas Dutoit and Outi Pasanen (New York: Fordham University Press, 2005), 1–64, here 59. For a fuller bibliographical note, see Chapter 1, note 27. Of course, remotivations of the sign *shibboleth* are always possible. A marginal note in one of the manuscripts of the Targum of Judges

offers this fascinating exchange in two languages: "[in Hebrew] 'Please say Shibboleth!' [in Aramaic]: 'Say now that the foreign worship is worn out.' But he said 'Although it is old, it is not worn out' and he did not want to speak according to [the former demand]. So they would seize him and slaughter him at the ford of the Jordan." Willem F. Smelik, *The Targum of Judges* (Leiden: E. J. Brill, 1995), 559. Smelik notes Midrashic parallels in which the Ephraimites are described as unable to pronounce *shibboleth* because they were idolaters attached to the cult of Baal (or Bel or Bul); the word triggered their routine of saying "lift up the idol Bel," since, by the principle of notarikon (the use of acronyms), *shibboleth* contains the name of the idol among its syllables: 'S *a'* *Bel*, "Lift up the idol Bel" (559–560).

7. One of the topoi of post-1970s literary and cultural theory, the idea of the "discursively constructed body" has often inspired reductive oppositions between a prelinguistic body versus a linguistically constructed one. Often the problem is a misleading conception of "language" as a sovereign instance; I shall be saying a little more later about the inherent plurality and non-identity of language. Careful thinkers have tried to honor the complexity of the question of the "body" in various ways. Judith Butler comments that although "the body is given through language, it is never fully given that way . . . it is as it were given and withheld at the same time, and language might be said to perform both of these operations." See Butler, *Senses of the Subject* (New York: Fordham University Press, 2015), 20. For a lucid and forceful overview of the language-reality (Symbolic-Real) problematic in Lacan (is the "real" a traumatic kernel exterior to the symbolic order, or a lack produced by that order?), see Charles Shepherdson, *Lacan and the Limits of Language* (New York: Fordham University Press, 2008). The body, like the "real" of which it is often the privileged figure, resists being understood either as natural or discursive: "it is a peculiar structure or phenomenon that is not governed by nature, but is at the same time irreducible to the symbolic order" (41). I discuss "the body" as figure in *The Politics of Aesthetics: Nationalism, Gender, Romanticism* (Stanford: Stanford University Press, 2003).

8. Jacques Derrida, "White Mythology: Metaphor in the Text of Philosophy," in *Margins of Philosophy*, trans. Alan Bass (Chicago: University of Chicago Press, 1978), 207–221.

9. Jean-Jacques Rousseau, *Essay sur l'origine des langues*, in *Oeuvres complètes*, (Paris: Hachette, 1909), 1:370: "La parole distingue l'homme entre les animaux: le langage distingue les nations entre elles: on ne connoît d'où est un homme qu'après qu'il a parlé."

10. The reference is to William Faulkner, *Absalom, Absalom!* (New York: Library of America, 1990), 115; for discussion, see Chapter 1. We shall return shortly to *Absalom, Absalom!*, but it may be noted that a wavering between fine shades of perception and crazed stereotyping seems inherent to all discourses of passing and policing. The literature concerned with nineteenth- and twentieth-century African American "passing" records an intense degree of (white) hysteria that derived at least in part from the ferocity with which the difference between white and black had been legally and culturally constructed. Near the beginning of Nella Larsen's *Passing*, during a complex scene in which two characters who are both "passing" see and weigh each other, the main character reflects, scornfully and nervously: "Did that woman, could that woman, somehow know that here before her very eyes . . . was a Negro? Absurd! Impossible! White people were so stupid about such things, for all that they usually asserted that they were able to tell; and by the most ridiculous means, fingernails, palms of hands, shapes of ears, teeth, and equally silly rot. They always took her for an Italian, a Spaniard, a Mexican or a gipsy." Nella Larsen, *Passing* (1929), ed. Carla Kaplan (New York: Norton, 2007), 10–11.

11. Jacques Derrida, "Afterword: Toward an Ethic of Discussion," in *Limited Inc*, trans. Samuel Weber and Jeffrey Mehlman (Evanston, IL: Northwestern University Press, 1988), 119.

12. Gobineau goes so far as to claim that the Jews have no native language at all, having borrowed a dialect from the Canaanites. "In their everyday life, however, the Jews used the tongue of the country where they settled; and further, these exiles were known everywhere by their special accent [*leur accent particulier*]. They

never succeeded in fitting their vocal organs to their adopted language, even when they had learnt it from childhood. [*Le langage qu'ils avaient adopté et appris dès la première enfance ne réussit jamais à assouplir leur organe vocal.*]" Arthur de Gobineau, *De l'inégalité des races humaines* (1853), ed. Hubert Juin (Paris: Editions Pierre Belfond, 1967), 195; *The Inequality of Human Races*, trans. Adrian Collins (Torrance, CA: The Noontide Press, 1983), 194. The most lurid document in this ugly genre is Wagner's diatribe "Judaism in Music." Like Gobineau, Wagner claims that the Jew "speaks the modern European languages merely as learnt, and not as mother tongues (*angeborene Sprachen*). . . . Throughout an intercourse of two millennia with European nations, culture has not succeeded in breaking the remarkable stubbornness of the Jewish disposition as regards the peculiarities of Semitic pronunciation. The first thing that strikes our ear as thoroughly foreign and unpleasant is a hissing, shrilling, buzzing and blundering expression of sound in the Jew's way speaking (*ein zischender, schrillender, summsender und murksender Lautausdruck der jüdischen Sprechweise*); add thereto an employment of words in a sense quite foreign to our nation's tongue, and an arbitrary twisting of the structure of our phrases—and this mode of speaking acquires at once the character of an intolerably jumbled blabber (*eines unerträglich verwirrten Geplappers*)." Richard Wagner, "Das Judenthum in der Musik" (1850), online at https://archive.org/details/Wagner-Richard-Das-Judentum-in-der-Musik (accessed June 6, 2016); "Judaism in Music," in *Richard Wagner's Prose Works*, trans. William Ashton Ellis (New York: Broude Brothers, 1966), 3:79–122, here 84, translation modified. The Nazis broke with *völkisch* linguisticism in favor of "blood," as Philippe Lacoue-Labarthe and Jean-Luc Nancy observe. See "The Nazi Myth," trans. Brian Holmes, *Critical Inquiry* 16, no. 2 (Winter 1990): 291–312, esp. 308ff.

13. References to Jephthah's oath and sacrifice of his daughter are found throughout the early modern European literary tradition, e.g., in *Hamlet* 2:2, where Hamlet provokes Polonius: "O Jephthah judge of Israel, what a treasure hadst thou?" See Péter Dávidházi, "'O Jephthah, Judge of Israel': From Original to Accreted

Meanings in Hamlet's Allusion," in *Shakespeare Survey 68: Shakespeare, Origins, and Originality*, ed. Peter Holland (Cambridge: Cambridge University Press, 2015), 48–61, for an illuminating discussion of this passage in *Hamlet* and the Jephthah topos generally. As Dávidházi's title indicates, Hamlet is quoting from a popular ballad rather than directly from the Geneva Bible, and he is drawing on a context in which the rashness of Jephthah's oath and the impiety of his keeping it was a commonplace of the era (see *Henry IV Part 3*, 5:1:92–94: "Perhaps thou wilt object my holy oath./To keep that oath were more impiety/Than Jephthah when he sacrificed his daughter"). Dávidházi also helpfully reminds us of the grisly details that sacrifice involves (the animal is flayed, dismembered, burned) and the various implied transgressions involved in sacrificing a daughter (since only certain animals, and of these only males, are proper sacrifices) (54, 58).

14. Jacques Lacan, *Four Fundamental Concepts of Psychoanalysis*, Seminar XI, trans. Alan Sheridan (New York: Norton, 1981), 275; *Les quatre concepts fondamentaux de la psychanalyse* (Paris: Seuil, 1973), 305–306.

15. Jacques Derrida, *Rogues: Two Essays on Reason*, trans. Pascale-Anne Brault and Michael Nass (Stanford: Stanford University Press, 2005), 101.

16. See the substantial entry for *patah* in the *Theological Dictionary of the Old Testament*, trans. David E. Green and Douglas W. Stott (Grand Rapids, MI: Eerdmans, 2003), 12:173–191. It is not clear whether the second meaning of the homonym involves a separate root; see 174–175. Typically, male names in the Bible record God's agency, and Jephthah's name follows this pattern as a verbal form with the subject implied: "he [God] opens [the womb]." As the story develops, Jephthah's name obtains ironic resonance insofar as he opens his mouth to an oath that *closes* his daughter's womb. Adi Ophir has commented to me that, unlike most of the biblical names with God as implied subject (Joshua, Nehemiah, Isaiah, etc.), "in the case of Yyftakh, the name sounds exactly like the verb in the future, male, singular tense" (personal communication). In other words, the pronunciation suggests "he will open": a name that allows for the possibility that

the bearer of the name is usurping God as the agent inscribed in the name (though "agency" is perhaps no longer applicable to such "opening," since such agency would be at work in its own name). Here and elsewhere, I thank Saul Olyan and Tammi Schneider, in addition to Adi Ophir, for their expert philological guidance through the complexities of biblical scholarship. Any mistakes are entirely my responsibility—above all my risky effort to discover in Jephthah's name the shadow of the homonym "to inscribe," and to read the name as self-damaging. On this astral level of philological speculation, one is tempted to read the shibboleth massacre as an allegorical assault on Hebrew identity (insofar as the etymology of Hebrew is "the one who has crossed over," and the Ephraimites are being slain as they try to cross the Jordan).

17. James Joyce, *Ulysses*, ed. Hans Walter Gabler (New York: Vintage Books, 1986), 373. Joyce's gesture is arguably bolder in *Ulysses* than in *Finnegans Wake*, where he leaves the word formally intact, though he layers it with feminine and prophetic resonance through consonance and assonance, while splicing "s" into "sh" (as we will see Celan doing with yet greater poetic intensity): "So may this sybilette be our shibboleth that we may syllable her well." *Finnegans Wake* (Harmondsworth: Penguin, 1976), 267.

18. Jacques Derrida, *Monolingualism of the Other, or the Prosthesis of Origin*, trans. Patrick Mensah (Stanford: Stanford University Press, 1998), 65.

19. Jacques Derrida, *Memoires for Paul de Man*, rev. ed., trans. Cecile Lindsay et al. (New York: Columbia University Press, 1989), 15. The lectures composing *Memoires* were "written in January and February, 1984" (xi), and Derrida gave the lecture that became *Schibboleth: Pour Paul Celan* at the University of Washington in October 1984 (see the note on the flyleaf of the French edition of *Schibboleth*), which gives extra resonance to Derrida's invocation of a "password" here.

20. See *Hamlet* 1.1.145–147. Later in the first act, Hamlet reacts ironically to the unlocatability of the specter: *"Hic et ubique?* Then

we'll shift our ground" (1.5.164). Derrida writes powerfully about this and other scenes in *Specters of Marx: The State of the Debt, the Work of Mourning, and the New International*, trans. Peggy Kamuf (New York: Routledge, 1994).

21. Jacques Derrida, "Des tours de Babel," in *Difference in Translation*, ed. Joseph F. Graham (Ithaca, NY: Cornell University Press, 1985), 165–207 (English), 209–248 (French), here 170 (English), 214 (French). Derrida is developing, via Voltaire's commentary on the meaning of Babel (Ba, father; Bel, god) and the relevant lines in Genesis, a meditation on the functioning and translation of Babel as a proper name.

## 4. *Schibboleth*: Derrida

1. Peter Szondi, *Celan Studies* (1972), ed. Jean Bollack et al., trans. Susan Bernofsky with Harvey Mendelsohn (Stanford: Stanford University Press, 2003), 85.

2. Jacques Derrida, *Shibboleth: For Paul Celan*, in *Sovereignties in Question: The Poetics of Paul Celan*, ed. Thomas Dutoit and Outi Pasanen (New York: Fordham University Press, 2005), 1–64, here 17. For a fuller bibliographical note, see Chapter 1, note 27.

3. Paul Celan, *The Meridian*, trans. Jerry Glenn, included as an appendix to Derrida, *Sovereignties in Question*, 173–185, here 180, translation modified. For the German original, see *Gesammelte Werke* (Frankfurt am Main: Suhrkamp, 1983), 3:187–202, here 196. Further references to *Der Meridian* are to these editions and are given parenthetically, in the order German/English (and I shall give the title in German form). Reference will also be made in what follows to the superb critical edition, *Der Meridian: Endfassung, Vorstufen, Materiellen*, ed. Bernard Böschenstein and Heino Schmull, with Michael Schwarzkopf and Christiane Wittkop (Frankfurt am Main: Suhrkamp, 1999); *The Meridian: Final Version—Drafts—Materials*, trans. Pierre Joris (Stanford: Stanford University Press, 2011); citations will be indicated as Böschenstein and Schmull, with pagination given German/English when necessary (since the pagination is the same up

to the appendix, only one page number will be given in most cases).

4. Celan is undoubtedly quoting from Fritz Bergemann's edition of Büchner, *Sämtliche Werke und Briefe* (Leipzig: Insel Verlag, 1922, last reprinted in 1956), which he owned (see Böschenstein and Schmull, 226/227), and which gives the opening sentence as "Den 20. Jänner ging Lenz durch's Gebirg" on the authority of Johann Friedrich Oberlin's *Aufzeichnungen*, which was also a major source for Büchner when he was writing the unfinished novella. For discussion see Walter Hinderer, *Büchner Kommentar zum dichterischen Werk* (Munich: Winkler Verlag, 1977), 158–163. One imagines that Celan knew full well that he was countersigning an editorial insertion with "Jänner," particularly given that later in *Der Meridian* he takes careful, if complicated note of an error made by Karl Emil Franzos, editor of the first critical edition of Büchner in 1879 (201–202/184). For an excellent discussion of *Der Meridian* that examines the reference to Franzos along with many other moments in the text, see Michael G. Levine, *A Weak Messianic Power: Figures of a Time to Come in Benjamin, Derrida, and Celan* (New York: Fordham University Press, 2014), 53–62.

5. Derrida, whose own writing displays a tenacious interest in dates, atypically missed the fact, while writing *Shibboleth*, that January 20 was the date of the Wannsee Conference, a fact of which Celan was inescapably aware, as Derrida notes when he comments on this matter in the section of his 2001–2002 seminar The *Beast and the Sovereign* that is excerpted as "Majesties" in *Sovereignties in Question* (see his remarks at 112–113). Since, as we know, Derrida's reflections in *Shibboleth* turn on the "double edge of a shibboleth" whereby "the mark of a covenant" also opens possibilities of "exclusion, discrimination, indeed, even of extermination" (63), his comments are if anything strengthened by the shadow cast over Celan's invocations of this date in *The Meridian*.

6. Philippe Lacoue-Labarthe, *Poetry as Experience*, trans. Andrea Tarnowski (Stanford: Stanford University Press, 1999), 18.

7. Jacques Derrida, "Autoimmunity: Real and Symbolic Suicides: A Dialogue with Jacques Derrida," in Giovanna Borradori,

*Philosophy in a Time of Terror: Dialogues with Jürgen Habermas and Jacques Derrida* (Chicago: University of Chicago Press, 2003), 85–136. I discuss this interview as part of an extended reflection on the name-date "9/11" in *The Rhetoric of Terror: Reflections on 9/11 and the War on Terror* (New York: Fordham University Press, 2009), esp. 1–48.

8. Echoing here the famous lines from "Aschenglorie," "Niemand/zeugt für den/Zeugen" (no one bears witness for the witness), Derrida, both in his reading of Celan and in other contexts, offers the figure of ash for the absolute finitude of the poem, the date, the trace, and what we call life. For a sustained meditation on extinction and poetry from a different archive, see Jacques Khalip, *Last Things* (New York: Fordham University Press, 2018).

9. Hent de Vries, "The Shibboleth Effect: On Reading Paul Celan," in *Judeities: Questions for Jacques Derrida*, ed. Joseph Cohen and Raphael Zagury-Orly (New York: Fordham University Press, 2007), 175–213, here 211.

10. Jacques Derrida, *Of Grammatology*, trans. Gayatri Chakravorty Spivak (Baltimore: Johns Hopkins University Press, 1976), 69.

11. Dates are cathected with equal intensity by revolutionary and reactionary forces in the modern era and can become visibly complex sites of political contestation, foreclosure, and memorialization. See my *Rhetoric of Terror*, as cited in note 7 above. In a German context, for instance, the date of November 9 summons a string of events: the proclamation of the Weimar Republic in 1918; Hitler's so-called Beer Hall Putsch in 1923; the *Kristallnacht* pogrom in 1938; and the fall of the Berlin Wall in 1989. (Well-informed German nationalists can add the execution of revolutionary leader Robert Blum in Vienna in 1848.) Two of these four (or five) events did not fall randomly on November 9. The Nazis were nothing if not attentive to dates, and the putsch and the pogrom were scheduled to overwrite the November Revolution.

12. William Faulkner, *Absalom, Absalom!* (New York: Library of America, 1990), 206.

13. John T. Matthews, "Recalling the West Indies: From Yoknapatawpha to Haiti and Back," *American Literary History* 16,

no. 2 (2004): 238–262. Matthews notes that although the Haitian Constitution of 1804 had abolished slavery and outlawed white ownership of land, "the *jaunes*, the 'yellow aristocracy,' succeeded the white French aristocracy and presided over a subdivision between *noirs* and *mulâtres*. . . . The renewal of racial oppression led to a series of bloody revolts by blacks in Haiti, the worst in 1848" (253). Indeed, in 1826, that is, just a year before Faulkner has Sutpen have his Haitian adventure, President Jean Pierre Boyer had put into effect the notorious Rural Code, which effectively reenslaved the (mainly dark-skinned) plantation workers by binding them to the land (253). Matthews's article, which forms part of a surge of scholarly interest in the relationship of the American South to the Caribbean (and it is of note that Faulkner wrote his novel in the wake of the two-decade-long U.S. occupation of Haiti, 1915–1934), speculates interestingly on numerous obscurities of the Sutpen story—the source of Sutpen's initial capital, for instance (spoils from the first marriage? but Matthews points to some inconsistencies) or of his French Creole–speaking black workers (who, Matthews notes, are endlessly referred to as "wild niggers" but never as *slaves*). One can read the novel as suggesting that Sutpen might have been engaged in illegal slave trading as well as other crimes. Such speculations build on the novel's portrayal of Sutpen as a borderline-illegal avatar of white (or: "white") male violence, forcing his way up the class and caste hierarchy.

14. The novel ends with one of the narrating characters, Shreve, generalizing the Sutpen predicament into apocalyptic race-hysteria: "I think that in time the Jim Bonds are going to conquer the western hemisphere. Of course it wont quite be in our time and of course as they spread toward the poles they will bleach out again like the rabbits and the birds do, so they wont show up so sharp against the snow. But it will still be Jim Bond; and so in a few thousand years, I who regard you will also have sprung from the loins of African kings" (311). The one-drop-of-blood rule of American antebellum race law generates (and arguably responds to) this kind of hysteria. Sutpen is the tail of the tornado (and a full analysis of the text would need to explore

in detail the construction of Sutpen as an over- and underdetermined pseudo-patriarch), but hints of potential racial ambiguity show up everywhere in *Absalom! Absalom!*, no matter how respectably "white" the character—all it takes is for evening to fall for Quentin Compson's father's hand to look "almost as dark as a negro's against his linen leg" (74). It is crucial for the plot, of course, that Charles Bon's, and for that matter, his mother Eulalia Bon's, African ancestry be invisible. Along with much paranoid writing, there is some sly humor in this vein: Sutpen's second wife, Ellen, is the daughter of "Goodhue" Coldfield.

15. Derrida's rich reflections in *On Touching—Jean-Luc Nancy*, trans. Christine Irizarry (Stanford: Stanford University Press, 2005), are valuable here. Although touch, as tact, will barely touch, indeed, *not* touch ("it touches what it does not touch" [67]), the touch cannot be isolated from the blow, or the blow from the caress: "a caress may be a blow and vice-versa" (69). *Absalom! Absalom!* illustrates precisely that latter case in the third of the three scenes in the novel in which the word shibboleth appears, when Sutpen puts his hand on Rosa's head (see Chapter 1, note 17).

16. Levine, *A Weak Messianic Power*, 65–66. Levine offers a detailed discussion of Derrida on circumcision, and a fine close reading of the one poem in which Celan uses that word, "Einem, der vor der Tür stand."

17. Celan, "Antwort auf eine Umfrage der Librairie Flinker" (1961), in *Gesammelte Werke* 3:175; "Reply to a Questionnaire from the Flinker Bookstore, Paris, 1961," in *Paul Celan: Collected Prose*, trans. Rosemarie Waldrop (Riverdale-on-Hudson, NY: Sheep Meadow Press, 1986), 23, translation modified, mainly so as to capture more literally the phrase *schicksalhaft Einmalige der Sprache* (Waldrop renders it: "by necessity a unique instance of language"). The question posed by Martin Flinker concerned bilingualism—whether a true poet could in fact write in more than one language. Celan's response (which picks up on Flinker's remark that in French the word *langue*, like "tongue" in English, means both language and a body part) is one of several texts that critics sometimes read as an indirect comment on the "Goll affair,"

since Yvan Goll, whose work Celan was accused (slanderously, by the widowed Claire Goll) of having plagiarized, was a "bilingual" poet who wrote in German and French. On the Goll affair, see Chapter 6, note 8.

## 5. Schibboleth: Celan

1. Celan wrote on October 3, 1954, to Isac Chiva: "I would be very glad to know what you think of [these poems] and above all what you think of the one I have named 'Schibboleth' (that is a word of Hebraic origin from the Old Testament; in German it means more or less 'recognition sign' ['*Erkennungszeichen*']), and in which, as you will see, I have inscribed the memory of the worker's uprising in Vienna and in revolutionary Madrid." The original is in French (and will be given later in this study); this is my translation of the extract provided in Barbara Wiedemann's apparatus to Celan's "Schibboleth." See Paul Celan, *Die Gedichte: Neue kommentierte Gesamtausgabe in einem Band*, ed. Barbara Wiedemann (Frankfurt am Main: Suhrkamp, 2018), 728. Further quotations from Celan's poetry are from Wiedemann's edition unless otherwise specified; her commentary will be cited parenthetically as "Wiedemann" plus page number. Translations are my own, since it has seemed useful in this context to provide, however awkwardly, line-by-line and when possible word-for-word correspondence.

2. Dollfuss, who belonged to the right-wing Christian Socialist party, became chancellor in May 1932, acquired dictatorial powers in March 1933, and established a one-party state along the lines of Italian fascism. He destroyed the socialist opposition in February 1934; five months later, Nazi conspirators assassinated him. The Mussolini-style *Austrofascismus* that Dollfuss had developed remained intact, with his successor Kurt Schuschnigg ruling largely by diktat until the *Anschluss* in 1938.

3. There will always be more possibilities, and one will never know to what extent the shibboleth has retreated into its secret. Andrea Timár has reminded me that the Red Army liberated Budapest on February 13, 1945. Michael Levine points plausibly

to "the *Action Française*'s attempted assassination of Leon Blum, leader of the *Front Populaire*, on February 13, 1936." Michael G. Levine, *A Weak Messianic Power: Figures of a Time to Come in Benjamin, Derrida, and Celan* (New York: Fordham University Press, 2014), 20. The bombing of Dresden on February 13–15, 1945, has also been nominated as a possible referent: see Marlies Janz, *Vom Engagement absoluter Poesie: Zur Lyrik und Ästhetik Paul Celans* (Frankfurt am Main: Syndikat, 1976), 153. That seems a stretch to me, but such stretching forms part of the challenge of reading Celan.

4. This reference is mentioned in most commentaries: see, e.g., Wiedemann, 821. One of the early drafts of "In Eins" adds street names that reinforce this interpretation: "Mit/dir, peuple de/Paris, vom/Boulevard du Temple bis/zur Rue du Chemin Vert. No pasarán." Paul Celan, *Werke: Historisch-Kritische Ausgabe*, 2nd ed., ed. Axel Gellhaus et al. (Frankfurt am Main: Suhrkamp, 2001), 6:233. Wiedemann notes that Celan scribbled "13 Februar 1962" onto a Communist Party flyer titled *Hommage aux martyres du 8 février 1962*; the flyer closes with the call: "VIVE LA LIBERTÉ! LE FASCISME NE PASSERA PAS!"

5. This second reference for "Dreizehnter Feber" is mentioned by most critics, including Derrida, but so far as I know I am adding my bit to the scholarly archive here in pointing to the headlines. Reproductions of the front pages of *Le Populaire* and *Le Breton Socialiste* for February 13, 1934, may be found at https://bataillesocialiste.wordpress.com. The demonstration of February 12, which drew together an otherwise splintered Left, was in response to the violent far-right rally of February 6, which was perceived by many as an attempt at a fascist coup d'état.

6. Jacques Derrida, *Shibboleth: For Paul Celan*, in *Sovereignties in Question: The Poetics of Paul Celan*, ed. Thomas Dutoit and Outi Pasanen (New York: Fordham University Press, 2005), 1–64, here 23. For a fuller bibliographical note, see Chapter 1, note 27.

7. As recorded in the lines quoted above, the word appears correctly accented in the later poem "In Eins." The falling-out of the accent in "Schibboleth," a small mark of contingency, is a mistake that Celan discovered a few years after the publication of

*Von Schwelle zu Schwelle* and corrected in some reprints; see Wiedemann, 637, as well as the commentary to "Schibboleth" by the editors of the Tübinger Ausgabe of *Von Schwelle zu Schwelle*, ed. Heino Schmull with Christiane Braun and Markus Heilman (Frankfurt am Main: Suhrkamp, 2002), 97. The mistake (if that is what it is) is an odd one, because Celan was nothing if not attentive to accents: he gave the acute, grave, and circumflex accents honored roles as metaphors for temporal states base on their properties of length in *Der Meridian*. See Paul Celan, *Gesammelte Werke* (Frankfurt am Main: Suhrkamp, 1983), 3:187–202, here 190; *The Meridian*, trans. Jerry Glenn, in Derrida, *Sovereignties in Question*, 173–185, here 175. Subsequent references are to these editions and are given in the order German/English.

8. "The social revolution of the nineteenth century cannot draw its poetry from the past but only from the future." Karl Marx, *The Eighteenth Brumaire of Louis Napoleon* (New York: International Publishers, 1963), 18. I was reminded of this resonant remark by Jan Mieszkowski's discussion of it in his fine article, "What's in a Slogan?" *Meditations* 29, no. 2 (Spring 2016): 149–160. Mieszkowski focuses on the rich history of slogans and reflection on slogans in the Marxist tradition from Marx himself through Luxemburg, Lenin, and Lukács. Though suspicious of empty phrases (the slogan as *Phrase* or *Parole*), Marx was of course one of history's great phrasemakers, and Mieszkowski offers a careful reading of Marx's effort, in his written praxis, to detach his pointed formulations from "a bourgeois discourse of investment and return or equivalence" (154).

9. I thank Thomas Schestag for alerting me to the transitive meaning of *erwacht*, as given in Grimm: "*tr.*, wie durchwachen: oft dann habe ich mit schlummer die längernden tage gekürzt, dich zu erwachen, o nacht, die du mir brachtest ein glück. Rückert 269, ges. ged. 2, 275, *dich wachend zu erreichen, nicht zu verschlafen.*" Schestag also reminds me of Faust's use of a similar word in his great opening monologue: "O sähst du, voller Mondenschein, /Zum letztenmal auf meine Pein, /Den ich so manche Mitternacht/An diesem Pult herangewacht . . ." (386–389).

10. Counting "Aurora" as Latin, "Petropolis" as Greek, and "toskanisch" as a Germanic modification of a Russian noun *toska* (see the following note), though part of the point is the inadequacy of these names for discreet languages in the face of words that drift among languages as names, loanwords, calques, etymological roots, and so on. In early drafts, Celan experimented with a phrase in Romanian as well: "Si de pe la voi mai sînt" (*Werke*, vol. 6.2, 234). This phrase remains, to me at least, a mystery. Since *sînt* can be either first-person singular "I am" or third-person plural "they are," the translation reads roughly either: "from among you or your parts (region) I am"; or, "from among you or your parts (region) there are." I thank Silvia Cernea Clark for her linguistic expertise and her extensive effort to contextualize this phrase, which neither she nor another native speaker and scholar whom she consulted, Gabriela Obodariu, could identify as a slogan or saying or quotation, though they hear an echo of biblical verses such as John 13:33: "yet a little while I am with you" (in Romanian: "mai sunt putin cu voi"), or John 14:25: "being yet present with you" ("cat mai sunt cu voi"). However unclear its intent, the phrase does seem to be evoking the lacerated terrain of the shibboleth ("I am of you and your region"; "there are others among you in your region").

11. Mandelstam refers to St. Petersburg as "Petropolis" in various poems, including one from the collection *Tristia* (1922) that Celan translated: "Petropolis, diaphane: hier gehen wir zugrunde" (5:93); for an English translation see *The Complete Poetry of Osip Emilevich Mandelstam*, ed. Sidney Monas, trans. Burton Raffel and Alla Burago (Albany: SUNY Press, 1973): "We'll die in transparent Petropolis" (91). *Toskanisch* relays a Mandelstamian pun that associates longing or melancholy *toska*, with Tuscany— *Toskana* in Russian, as in German: the land from which Dante was exiled, and toward which Mandelstam also inclined. See his poem "Don't make comparisons—the living are incomparable" from the *Second Voronezh Notebook* (1937): "But this clear anguish [*toska*] will not let me go / Away from the youthful hills of Voronezh / To the civilized hills, that I see so clearly in Tuscany."

*The Voronezh Notebooks*, trans. Richard and Elizabeth McKane (Newcastle upon Tyne: Bloodaxe Books, 1996), 66. (Mandelstam spent a period of exile in Voronezh; that is at least one reason why Petropolis is the "wandering city of the unforgotten" in Celan's poem.) For more on this pun, see Clare Cavenagh, *Osip Mandelstam and the Modernist Creation of Tradition* (Princeton, NJ: Princeton University Press, 1995), 275–277. For a general discussion of Celan and Mandelstam, see Anna Glazova, "Poetry of Bringing About Presence: Paul Celan Translates Osip Mandelstam," *MLN* 124 (2009): 1108–1126. The band taken from the eyes also alludes to Mandelstam, inverting a line in "Oh, this slow asthmatic vastness": "Give me a blindfold over my eyes/When the horizon recovering its breath is wide open" (*The Voronezh Notebooks*, 65). I thank Luba Golburt for pointing me to the poem "Don't make comparisons" and to Glazova's article, over the course of a detailed discussion of Mandelstam's importance for Celan. These lines from "In Eins" do not *just* refer to Mandelstam, of course. Janz points out, for instance (153), that "Petropolis" cues the Brazilian city in which Stefan Zweig and his wife lived for two years before taking their lives in 1942—another story of a poet in exile to accompany those of Mandelstam and Celan (and those of Dante and Ovid that Mandelstam so often evokes).

12. On the French source for Büchner's phrase, see Wiedemann, 823. The *Hessische Landbote* was written by Büchner but revised by Friedrich Ludwig Weidig; the pamphlet was secretly distributed on the night of July 31, 1834, in Hesse-Darmstadt. When the identities of the authors were discovered, Büchner was able to flee to France; Weidig was arrested and committed suicide, possibly with the collusion of the authorities, after suffering mistreatment in prison. The eight-page pamphlet is one of the most radical political documents of the so-called Vormärz period, the years leading up to the 1848 revolution.

13. Abadias (as rendered in English, Obadiah: "servant of God") is a name that, like a date, bears the trace of a singular encounter (Celan knew a refugee from Huesca who bore this name: see Wiedemann, 822) while opening the possibility of

other relays. There are several Obadiahs in the Bible, but no specific allusion seems intended.

14. The difficult, aporetic thought pursued in their different ways by Derrida and Celan is that the poem is *exposed* in its singularity to iterability as a condition of its (im)possibility. Celan writes of poetic images in *Der Meridian*: "That which is perceived and to be perceived one time, one time over and over again [*das einmal, das immer wieder einmal*], and only now and only here" (199/183).

15. Hands play an important role in Celan's poetic vocabulary, as suggested by his evocation of the lines from "Stimmen" about walking on hands in *Der Meridian*. There is also this famous remark in the "Letter to Hans Bender": "Craft means handiwork, a matter of hands. And these hands must belong to *one* person, i.e. a unique, mortal soul searching for its way with its voice and its dumbness [*Stummheit*]. Only truthful hands write true poems. I cannot see any basic difference between a handshake [*Händedruck*] and a poem." "Brief an Hans Bender," *Gesammelte Werke* 3:177; "Letter to Hans Bender," *Paul Celan: Collected Prose*, 26.

16. The allusion is to the influential quasi-dialogue between Jean-Luc Nancy and Maurice Blanchot: see Nancy, *La communauté désoeuvrée* (Paris: Christian Bourgois, 1986), translated by Peter Connor as *The Inoperative Community* (Minneapolis: University of Minnesota Press, 1991); Blanchot, *La communauté inavouable* (Paris: Minuit, 1983), translated by Pierre Joris as *The Unavowable Community* (Barrytown, NY: Station Hill Press, 1988); most recently, Nancy, *La communauté désavouée* (Paris: Galilée, 2014), translated by Philip Armstrong as *The Disavowed Community* (New York: Fordham University Press, 2016). Blanchot's book is a response to Nancy's essay "La communauté, le nombre," *Aléa* (February 1983), which was revised and taken up in *La communauté désoeuvrée*.

17. Christopher Fynsk, *Language and Relation . . . that there is language* (Stanford: Stanford University Press, 1996), 153. "Heidegger, by introducing his concept of *Mitsein* ("being-with"), recognized the necessity of thinking Dasein in relation, but he failed to carry

through this concept in any manner adequate to his own description of the facticity of Dasein" (ibid.).

18. Celan's poetry infuses with great power the ancient trope of heart and word: nowhere more famously than during the legendary meeting with Heidegger in Heidegger's cabin, when Celan wrote into the guestbook: "Ins Hüttenbuch, mit dem Blick auf den Brunnenstern, mit einer Hoffnung auf ein kommendes Wort im Herzen. Am 25 Juli 1967. (signed) Paul Celan." As given in Otto Pöggeler, *Spur des Wortes: Zur Lyrik Paul Celans* (Freiburg: Verlag Karl Alber, 1986), 259: a translation would read: "In the cabin book, with a view toward the well-star, with the hope of a coming word in the heart.") *Brunnenstern*, or well-star, refers to a star motif on a wooden cube over the well by the hut, visible in old photographs; Celan developed the figure of "the well with the/star-die above it" in his great poem "Todtnauberg," a poem that hopes "for a thinker's/coming/word/in the heart." The allusion to Heidegger's silence about his past is inescapable, but Celan's phrase asks for far more than a confession, apology, or expression of penitence.

19. If "Peuple/de Paris" refers to a *peuple* from either 1962 or 1934, it could then with at least chronological verisimilitude have "Petropolis," as the city of the Russian revolution, lying as the "wandering city of the unforgotten" on its heart—a reading that is not without merit, given the poem's thematization of the remembering of revolutionary acts and speech acts, and its superimposition of places, languages, and times. The absurdity of the resultant image, however—a Parisian *peuple* with Petropolis *toskanisch* on its heart—suggests that we are probably better off letting these *dir*s go their separate way.

20. If we were intending to reconstruct Celan's intentions in a traditional way, we would have reason to claim that the poem's second "*dir*" gestures in the first instance toward Mandelstam. In one of the drafts lying behind this part of "In Eins," Celan copied the first line of Mandelstam's 1920 poem, "V Peterburge my soidemsia snova" ("In Petersburg we will meet again") in Cyrillic script as an epigraph (*Werke*, 6:231). I once again thank Luba Golburt for her help with this reference.

21. See note 12. The final line cannot be said to be "by" any single legally constituted "author": not Celan, but also not even Büchner, a fact that of course does not prevent individuals from suffering legal or extralegal violence; Weidig in a sense died for the text from which this line comes.

22. Kristina Mendicino, "An Other Rhetoric: Paul Celan's Meridian," *MLN* 126, no. 3 (2011): 630–650 (here 650). Citation is a dizzyingly dense topic in *Der Meridian*, since in deploying and troping on citations from Büchner, Celan is quoting an author whose texts are themselves notoriously laced with unacknowledged citation; of Büchner's massive incorporation of other texts, Helmut Müller-Sievers comments that "there really is no parallel case in the German tradition." See Helmut Müller-Sievers, "On the Way to Quotation: Paul Celan's 'Meridian' Speech," *New German Critique* 91 (2004): 131–149, here 139.

## 6. "S(ch)ibboleth": Apostrophe

1. My readings in the German and English archive have turned up numerous brief discussions of the poem that for the most part explain the "Februar" and "No pasarán" allusions and then move on to other texts; see, e.g., Marlies Janz, *Vom Engagement absoluter Poesie: Zur Lyrik und Ästhetik Paul Celans* (Frankfurt am Main: Syndikat, 1976), 152–153; Peter Horst Neumann, *Zur Lyrik Paul Celans* (Göttingen: Vandenhoeck & Ruprecht, 1968), 58–60; or even, despite the title of his chapter and book, Theo Buck, "'Schibboleth' oder: Die Identifikation mit dem Spanischen Bürgerkrieg," in *Schibboleth: Konstelationen um Celan* (Aachen: Rimbaud, 1996), 9–28. Buck provides useful literary-historical context for Celan's investment in the Spanish Civil War but offers little formal analysis either of "Schibboleth" or "In Eins." A helpful collation of the standard references and explanations for "In Eins" is to be found in Thomas Spurr's entry "In Eins," in *Kommentar zu Paul Celans 'Die Niemandrose'*, ed. Jürgen Lehmann (Heidelberg: C. Winter, 1997), 270–276. Michael Levine's rich discussion of "In Eins" has been noted; he does not discuss the poem "Schibboleth," although he does have a

fine sentence on the word *shibboleth* as "used above all to describe words unconsciously proffered and silently tendered; words that come only by accident and in place of others." Michael G. Levine, *A Weak Messianic Power: Figures of a Time to Come in Benjamin, Derrida, and Celan* (New York: Fordham University Press, 2014), 11. The most extended discussion of the poem "Schibboleth" that I have found is not in Celan studies per se but in Ulrike Bail, "Ein Wort als Grenze: Schibbolet," in *Dem Tod nicht glauben: Sozialgeschichte der Bibel*, ed. Frank Crüsemann et al. (Gütersloh: Gütersloh Verlagshaus, 2004), 293–311. Bail is interested in Celan's deliberate "distortion" of the biblical story, which "makes clear that the shibboleth can also function as password (*Losungswort*) in the fight against discrimination, selection, deadly unambiguousness (*Eindeutigkeit*) and exclusion" (307–308).

2. Jacques Derrida, *Shibboleth: For Paul Celan*, in *Sovereignties in Question: The Poetics of Paul Celan*, ed. Thomas Dutoit and Outi Pasanen (New York: Fordham University Press, 2005), 1–64, here 30. For a fuller bibliographical note, see Chapter 1, note 27.

3. Evoking here the extraordinary afterlife of Benjamin's early essay "On Language as Such and the Language of Men" (1916): "the impart*able* is immediately language itself" ("dieses Mitteil*bare* ist unmittelbar die Sprache selbst"; Benjamin's emphasis). Walter Benjamin, *Gesammelte Schriften* (Frankfurt: Suhrkamp, 1980), 2:142; *Selected Writings, Vol. 1: 1913–1926*, ed. Marcus Bullock and Michael W. Jennings (Cambridge, MA: Harvard University Press, 1996), 64, translation modified per Samuel Weber's suggestion. On the translation of *mitteilen* as "impart," see Weber, *Benjamin's— abilities* (Cambridge, MA: Harvard University Press, 2008), 40–42. I return briefly to the endlessly rich question of translation later.

4. With regard to "Schibboleth," Celan commented to a friend that "not for nothing does this poem stand next to 'In memoriam Paul Eluard'": see Barbara Wiedemann's notes in Paul Celan, *Die Gedichte: Neue kommentierte Gesamtausgabe in einem Band*, ed. Barbara Wiedemann (Frankfurt am Main: Suhrkamp, 2018), 726–727. For some connections between "In Eins" and "Hinausgekrönt," see 823–824. Celan's poems are cited from this edition; references to the commentary will be given

parenthetically as "Wiedemann" plus page number. Translations are my own unless otherwise noted.

5. Peter Szondi, *Celan Studies* (1972), ed. Jean Bollack et al., trans. Susan Bernofsky with Harvey Mendelsohn (Stanford: Stanford University Press, 2003), 28; "Der Leser ist vom Anfang an *verbracht*—in eine fremde und fremdartige Gegend," *Celan-Studien* (Frankfurt am Main: Suhrkamp, 1972), 48, emphasis in the original. "Engführung" (1958) was collected in *Sprachgitter* (1959).

6. "Prisoners everywhere dreaded the quarries," as Nikolaus Wachsmann writes in his comprehensive *KL: A History of the Nazi Concentration Camps* (New York: Farrar, Straus and Giroux, 2015), 213. At Mauthausen, which was for some time the only "grade III" camp according to SS classification, the lethal quarries exemplified *Vernichtung durch Arbeit*, but the quarries at Gross-Rosen and Flossenbürg, the brickworks at Sachsenhausen, etc., also became infamous places in a nightmare geography (see Wachsmann, esp. 213–214).

7. Images of rock, stone, and architectural form appear throughout Mandelstam's work (his first collection is titled *Stone* [1913]); see, e.g., the important early essay "Morning of Acmeism," *Mandelstam: The Complete Critical Prose*, ed. Jane Gray Harris, trans. Jane Gray Harris and Constance Link (Ann Arbor, MI: Ardis Press, 1979), esp. 62. On Celan's deep engagement with Mandelstam's poetry, see, in addition to work cited earlier, Alexi Wolskij, "Über den Einfluss Ossip Mandelstam auf die Dichtung Paul Celans," *Akten des XI. Internationalen Germanistenkongresses* (Frankfurt am Main: Peter Lang, 2005), ed. Jean Marie Valentin, 219–220. On the importance of stone in Celan, see the discussion and notes later in this chapter.

8. For these and other fragmentary drafts, see Paul Celan, *Werke: Historisch-kritische Ausgabe*, ed. Holger Gehle et al. (Frankfurt am Main: Suhrkamp, 2004), 4.2:184–192. The last quotation is given as printed, with a parenthesis that does not close. If one considers the poem in the context of a biographical archive, these canceled lines are easily seen as relaying energies from the incipient "Goll affair." In a letter to his wife dated March 26, 1954, Celan recounts having for the first time seen, or at least been given

a full account of, the slanderous *Rundbrief* that Claire Goll began sending to chosen recipients in 1953, in which she for the first time brought charges of plagiarism against Celan into a semipublic realm. "Schibboleth" was probably composed a few months later (as noted earlier, the poem appears extant for the first time in Celan's letter of October 3, 1954, to Chiva). Celan no doubt discarded these lines for many reasons, aesthetic as well as personal; notably, when he "rewrote" "Schibboleth" as the more lapidary "In Eins," it was at the height of Claire Goll's public campaign against him, which began in April, 1960 and had its *Schwerpunkt*, as Barbara Wiedemann notes, in 1960–1962. Celan's response, as regards the sequence of poems we are studying here, was severely to purge away the drama of persecution—and indeed, to affirm, in the polyglot and polyphonic "In Eins," a poetico-political citationality that would give the lie in the profoundest sense to the malicious charges of plagiarism by which Celan, as we know, remained tormented for the rest of his life. For documents and commentary pertaining to the "Goll affair," see Barbara Wiedemann, *Paul Celan—Die Goll-Affäre: Dokumente zu einer "Infamie"* (Frankfurt am Main: Suhrkamp, 2000); see 226–239 for documentation pertaining to Celan's first encounter with the circulating letter.

9. Although not sufficiently activated by details in the poem to be strictly germane to an interpretation of it, the relatively minimal difference between the flags flown by the belligerents in the Spanish Civil War is perhaps worth footnoting, overshadowed as our memories of European fascism are by the dramatic iconography of National Socialism. The Republicans and Nationalists both drew on Spanish tradition and flew very similar flags—indeed, Franco's forces began by using the republican governmental flag, a tricolor of red, yellow, and *morado* (purple) with a coat of arms in the center. After the first month of the war the Nationalists omitted the purple and flew a two-color flag, a yellow stripe between two red stripes, reprising Bourbon colors. As noted, Celan's poem does not construct a scene detailed enough for us to say anything determinate about the flag in the marketplace; but it is helpful to keep in mind that the narrator's ferocious

rejection of it can always turn on a difference as minute and decisive as that between *shibboleth* and *sibboleth*.

10. The toponym Estremadura refers back to the Duero River and comes from a Celtic root, but the pun is traditional: *durus*, hard, harsh; *extremus*, uttermost, outermost, farthest, last. The borderland between Christians and Moors, this stony land may be read as evoking, in Celan's poem, the Abrahamic desert.

11. The poem also possibly alludes here to Celan's friend Erich Einhorn. Wiedemann is skeptical, pointing out that Celan had lost all contact with Eichhorn in the last years of the war; but given the density of autobiographical signing in Celan's poetry and the fact that Einhorn shared Celan's enthusiasm for the workers' uprising in Vienna and the Republican cause in Spain, no firm line can be drawn. On Celan and Eichhorn's youthful political engagement, see Israel Chalfen, *Paul Celan: Eine Biographie seiner Jugend* (Frankfurt am Main: Suhrkamp, 1979), 114. See also Marina Dmitrieva-Einhorn, "'Einhorn: du weißt um die Steine . . .': Zum Briefwechsel Paul Celans mit Erich Einhorn," *Celan Jahrbuch* 7 (1997–98) (Heidelberg: Universitäts-Verlag C. Winter, 1999), 7–22, with previously unpublished letters from her family archive, 23–49. Celan learned of Einhorn's address in Moscow in 1962 and renewed contact with him; the correspondence continues through 1967.

12. "Gott hat sie aus Egypten gefüret/seine freidigkeit ist wie eins Einhorns"; "Meinstu das Einhorn werde dir dienen/vnd werde bleiben an deiner krippen?"; "Hilff mir aus dem Rachen des Lewen/Vnd errette mich von den Einhörnern." The references are to Numbers (or in Luther's titling, the fourth book of Moses) 23:22; Job 39:9; and Psalm 22:22. In the King James Version the first two run: "God brought them out of Egypt: he hath as it were the strength of a unicorn"; and "Will the unicorn be willing to serve thee?" The King James translation of Psalm 22 is numbered and translated slightly differently: "Save me from the lion's mouth: for thou hast heard me from the horns of the unicorns" (22:21).

13. Paul Celan, *Gesammelte Werke* (Frankfurt am Main: Suhrkamp, 1983), 3:187–202, here 196; *The Meridian*, trans. Jerry

Glenn, in Derrida, *Sovereignties in Question*, 173–185, here 180. Subsequent references are to these editions, and are given in the order German/English.

14. See Paul Celan, *Der Meridian: Endfassung, Vorstufen, Materiellen*, ed. Bernard Böschenstein and Heino Schmull, with Michael Schwarzkopf and Christiane Wittkop (Frankfurt am Main: Suhrkamp, 1999), 98. Celan has a speaker say in "The Poetry of Osip Mandelstam," that Mandelstam's poetry is *"aktualisierte Sprache, stimmhaft und stimmlos zugleich" ("actualized* language, voiceful and voiceless simultaneously)" (215, emphasis in the original); and in the materials for *Der Meridian* we read: "Zu Kamen [which is Russian for stone, and, as noted is the title of Mandelstam's first collection]: Er spricht—er schweigt" (141). A reading of the figure of stone in Celan would need to traverse a great many texts, from the early poetry to important poems such as "Radix, Matrix" or "Ein Wurfholz" and the prose text "Gespräch im Gebirg," to the late work (e.g., "Rebleute graben"). Stone metaphors have characterized some famous impressionistic generalizations about Celan's language: Hans-Georg Gadamer writes of Celan's block-like speech, *blockhaftes Sprechen*, in "Sinn und Sinnverhüllung bei Paul Celan," *Gedicht und Gespräch* (Frankfurt am Main: Suhrkamp, 1990), 137; one also thinks of Adorno's famous comment that Celan's poems "imitate a language beneath the helpless language of human beings, indeed, beneath all organic language: it is that of the dead matter of stone and star [*des Toten von Stein und Stern*]": *Ästhetische Theorie, Gesammelte Schriften*, ed. Rolf Tiedemann et al. (Frankfurt am Main: Suhrkamp, 1977), 7:477; *Aesthetic Theory*, trans. Robert Hullot-Kentor (Minneapolis: University of Minnesota Press, 1997), 322, translation modified.

15. This in contrast to early poems such as "Halbe Nacht" or "Unstetes Herz" from *Mohn und Gedächtnis*, in which flutes have pastoral and erotic roles: "Die schwarze Flöte schnitzten sie uns aus lebendigem Holz" ("they whittle us the black flute out of living wood") ("Halbe Nacht").

16. The fall of Badajoz was a crucial early victory for the Nationalists, bringing them control of the Estremadura region

and opening the way to Madrid. Massacres were perpetrated on both sides, though systematically and on a vastly greater scale by Franco's forces, and the Badajoz massacre is probably the most famous of the mass killings that occurred as villages and towns were captured throughout the war. The Nationalist commander, Juan Yagüe, became known as the "Butcher of Badajoz" in the aftermath of the massacre, which was widely reported in the international press.

17. For the early drafts, see the Tübinger Ausgabe of *Von Schwelle zu Schwelle*, ed. Heino Schmull with Christiane Braun and Markus Heilman (Frankfurt am Main: Suhrkamp, 2002), 95–96.

18. Wiedemann notes that this is the first appearance of the word *Heimat* in the authorized poetry. As she remarks, it appears, always in complex ways, in several important subsequent poems, including "Radix, Matrix" (729). The publication of the magisterial *Bibliothèque philosophique*, a catalogue of Celan's annotations to philosophical books in his library, has recovered lines written on the endpaper of his copy of Jean Améry, *Jenseits von Schuld und Sühne*: "Heimat,— /Und ich? Ich war nicht einmal/zuhause als ich daheim/(zuhause) war" [Homeland,— /And I? I was never once/at home when I was home/(at home)]. *La bibliothèque philosophique/Die philosophische Bibliothek: Catalogue raisonné des annotations*, ed. Alexandra Richter, Patrik Alac, and Bertrand Badiou (Paris: Editions Rue d'Ulm, 2004), 459. For a study of the shattering of the name "Bukovina" the erased place of the *Heimat*, into letters scattered through Celan's life and texts, see Thomas Schestag, "buk," *MLN* 109, no. 3 (1994): 399–444.

19. Quintilian, *Instititio Oratoria* 4.1, trans. Donald A. Russell (Cambridge, MA: Harvard University Press, 2001), 210–211.

20. Jonathan Culler, "Apostrophe," *The Pursuit of Signs: Semiotics, Literature, Deconstruction* (New York: Routledge, 1981), 149–171, here 149.

21. Culler refers to Paul de Man's "Autobiography as De-Facement," originally published in *MLN* in 1979, but now most easily available in *The Rhetoric of Romanticism* (New York: Columbia University Press, 1984), 67–81. The relevant sentence

from de Man reads: "the latent threat that inhabits prosopopeia, namely that by making the death [*sic*] speak, the symmetrical structure of the trope implies, by the same token, that the living are struck dumb, frozen in their own death" (78).

22. Celan, *Gesammelte Werke*, 3:181. The epigram is dated March 26, 1969.

## 7. S(c)hibboleth: Babel

1. Israel Chalfen, *Paul Celan: Eine Biographie seiner Jugend* (Frankfurt am Main: Suhrkamp, 1979), 48.

2. "Ansprache anlässlich der Entgegennahme des Literaturpreises der Freien Hansestadt Bremen," *Gesammelte Werke* (Frankfurt am Main: Suhrkamp, 1983), 3:185–186; "Speech on the Occasion of Receiving the Literature Prize of the Free Hanseatic City of Bremen," in in *Paul Celan: Collected Prose*, trans. Rosemarie Waldrop (Riverdale-on-Hudson, NY: Sheep Meadow Press, 1986), 33–35, here 34, translation modified.

3. In "Silent Wine: Celan and the Poetics of Belatedness," *New German Critique* 91 (2004): 5–24, Michael G. Levine notes that Celan's text sets up a chiming sequence of "-reich" words (*Bedeutungsbereich, Klang des Unerreichbaren, das Erreichbare, das zu Erreichende, diese Erreichbarkeit*) as it moves toward "ange*reich*ert," thereby recording, Levine suggests, "the spectral grasp" of "the short-lived 'thousand-year Reich'" (15). See also Christopher Fynsk, *Language and Relation . . . that there is language* (Stanford: Stanford University Press, 1996), 136–141, for a careful reading of the Bremen speech as, among other things, an *Auseinandersetzung* with Heidegger. Language is *angereichert* in its passage through silence because it "now offers itself in its historicity and as the ground of a relation that is radically finite" (139).

4. Celan wrote to Ingeborg Bachmann (November 12, 1959) that the poem "Todesfuge" is "an epitaph and a grave. . . . My mother also has only *this* grave" ("eine Grabschrift und ein Grab. . . . Auch meine Mutter hat nur *dieses* Grab"). *Herzzeit: Ingeborg*

*Bachmann Paul Celan, Der Briefwechsel*, ed. Bertrand Badiou et al. (Frankfurt am Main: Suhrkamp, 2009), 127.

5. Thomas Schestag, "buk," *MLN* 109, no. 3 (1994): 405: "das Gedicht ist nicht sowohl *in* einer Sprache, *in* mehreren Sprachen geschrieben, als dass die Sprache, als dass Sprachen *ins* Gedicht einwandern."

6. Jacques Derrida, *Monolingualism of the Other* (Stanford: Stanford University Press, 1998), 61.

7. This on the authority of Barbara Wiedemann's commentary: see Paul Celan, *Die Gedichte: Neue kommentierte Gesamtausgabe in einem Band*, ed. Barbara Wiedemann (Frankfurt am Main: Suhrkamp, 2018), 728.

8. This is to suggest that the "German" word *Schibboleth* remains very slightly apart from the helpful discriminations of which Yasemin Yildiz reminds us in *Beyond the Mother Tongue: The Postmonolingual Condition* (New York: Fordham University Press, 2012): "[in German,] the *Fremdwort* is distinguished, on the one hand, from linguistically unintegrated foreign words and on the other hand, from words whose foreign origin is no longer perceived" (68). The ability to distinguish among these three categories is of course part of native competence—the foreigner, *der Fremde*, will not necessarily be able to perceive the *Fremdwort* for what it is.

9. "Fremdwörter sind die Juden der Sprache." *Minima Moralia: Reflexionen aus dem beschädigten Leben* (1951), in *Gesammelte Schriften* (Frankfurt am Main: Suhrkamp, 1980), 4:125; *Minima Moralia: Reflections from Damaged Life*, trans. E. F. N. Jephcott (New York: Verso, 2005), 110, translation modified.

10. "Über den Gebrauch von Fremdwörtern," in *Gesammelte Schriften* 11:640–646, here 644: the essay was written in the early 1930s and remained unpublished in Adorno's lifetime. "On the Use of Foreign Words," in *Notes to Literature II*, trans. Shierry Weber Nicholsen (Columbia University Press, 1992), 286–291, here 289.

11. "Wörter aus der Fremde" (1959), in *Gesammelte Schriften* 11:216–232, here 224; "Words from Abroad," *Notes to Literature I*,

trans. Shierry Weber Nicholsen (New York: Columbia University Press, 1991), 185–199, here 192, translation modified.

12. Carl Schmitt, *The Nomos of the Earth in the International Law of the Jus Publicum Europaeum* (1950), trans. G. L. Ulmen (New York: Telos Press, 2003), 67. Schmitt proposes to recover an "original spatial sense" for *nomos* that would be more archaic than custom or law: the verbal form *nemein* directs us toward primordial acts of appropriation, distribution, and production: to take (*nehmen*); to divide (*teilen*); to distribute (*verteilen*); to pasture (*weiden*).

13. Theodore Hiebert, "The Tower of Babel and the Origin of the World's Cultures," *Journal of Biblical Literature* 126, no. 1 (2007): 29–58, here 47.

14. Joseph Leo Koerner comments, in a more humanistic vein, and in the wake of a scrupulous analysis: "In Bruegel, humans are imaginative, energetic, and sociable, but they are also inherently confused. The tower built on the plain of Shinar was architecturally a Babel from the start." *Bosch & Bruegel: From Enemy Painting to Everyday Life* (Princeton, NJ: Princeton University Press, 2016), 304. Bruegel painted two versions of *The Tower of Babel*; I mainly have in mind the one in the Kunsthistorisches Museum in Vienna, but these broad remarks also apply to the smaller and probably slightly later painting in the Museum Boijmans Van Beuningen in Rotterdam.

15. One is reminded of the opening of Celan's famous "Psalm": "Niemand knetet uns wieder aus Erde und Lehm" ("No one will knead us again out of earth and mud") (Wiedemann, 132). Even more striking are the opening lines of a poem written a couple of years later (October 16, 1963) that eventually appeared in *Atemwende* (1967): "Von Ungeträumtem geätzt, / wirft das schlaflos durchwanderte Brotland / den Lebensberg auf. / Aus seiner Krume / knetest du neu unsre Namen . . ." ("Etched by the undreamed, / the sleeplessly wandered-through breadland casts / up the life-mountain. / Out of its crumb / you knead anew our names . . .") (Wiedemann, 179). It would be typical of Celan to have attended to the bread-making element in the verb *balal* in the Babel story. Another poem that would be worth reading

carefully in this context is the one that Celan placed directly after "In eins" in *Die Niemandsrose*, "Hinausgekrönt," in which the fierce *hin*-movement of the first word moves toward an evocation of Mandelstam's death in a penal camp, a massive reversal of heaven and earth and a refusal of Yahweh's descent: "Und wir schicken / keinen der Unsern hinunter / zu dir, / Babel" ("And we'll send / none of our people down / to you, / Babel").

16. Jacques Derrida, *Shibboleth: For Paul Celan*, in *Sovereignties in Question: The Poetics of Paul Celan*, ed. Thomas Dutoit and Outi Pasanen (New York: Fordham University Press, 2005), 1–64, here 28. For a fuller bibliographical note, see Chapter 1, note 27.

17. See Chapter 6, note 3 for the Benjamin citation and Samuel Weber's important study of "-abilities" (the "-bar" suffix that Benjamin himself italicizes in this particular quotation).

18. William Gibson, *Count Zero* (New York: Ace Books, 1986), 5.

19. And even in cruder scripts, plot elements involving language have a way of pressing past techno-fantasies of seamless translation. The "Universal Translator," for instance, that the Star Trek series inherits from earlier sci fi (and that invites interpretation as a figure for the late twentieth-century globalization of English, projected onto an Americanized galactic-sized future), not infrequently fails when the source language is Klingon.

20. The noise from heaven recalls Exodus 19:19: "Moses spake and God answered him with a voice" (the Hebrew *qol* can be variously "voice" or "thunder"). This terrifying manifestation then becomes "speaking" as God gives the Decalogue: "God spake" (20:1). "But to whom?" wonders Herbert Marks, the editor of the Norton *English Bible: The Old Testament* (New York: Norton, 2012): "(Moses alone? Moses in the people's hearing? the people directly?). . . . This is the only instance in the Hebrew Bible where the verb "to speak" is used without an indirect object" (148).

21. The reference here, of course, is to Aristotle's famous distinction between *phônê*, which all animals possess, and *logos*, thanks to which the human is the political animal, because partnership, *koinônia*, through *logos* composes household and *polis*, with the *polis*, as the whole over the parts, taking precedence over household and individual: see *Politics* 1.2, 1253a, 14–19.

22. In Acts, glossolalia appears twice as a gift of the Holy Ghost: "on the Gentiles also was poured out the gift of the Holy Ghost. For they heard them speak with tongues, and magnify God" (10:45–46); "And when Paul had laid his hands upon them, the Holy Ghost came on them, and they spake with tongues, and prophesied" (19:6). In 1 Corinthians 14, Paul registers ambivalence: though some of his comments lend encouragement to the idea of glossolalia as divine or angelic speech, his recommendation that translators be on hand suggests that he is talking about inspired worshippers falling back into some non-Greek ("barbarian") language or village dialect of their youth: "Therefore if I know not the meaning of the voice, I shall be unto him that speaketh a barbarian, and he that speaketh shall be a barbarian unto me. . . . Wherefore let him that speaketh in an unknown tongue pray that he may interpret" (14:11, 14:13). Paul inscribes himself in this uncertain dialectic: "I thank my God, I speak with tongues more than ye all: yet in the church I had rather speak five words with my understanding, that by my voice I might teach others also, than ten thousand words in an unknown tongue. . . . For God is not the author of confusion. . . . Wherefore, brethren, covet to prophecy and forbid not to speak with tongues" (14:18–19, 33, 39). It is perhaps not coincidental that Paul's notorious command (which is possibly a scribal insertion) "Let your women keep silence in the churches" appears in this context (14:34); the proximity of babel has perhaps raised, for Paul or for his scribe, the threatening specter of the feminine as a figure for linguistic excess.

23. Paul Celan, *Der Meridian*, *Gesammelte Werke*, 3:187–202, here 200; *The Meridian*, trans. Jerry Glenn, in Derrida, *Sovereignties in Question*, 173–185, here 183, translation modified. The sentence is hard to translate: "Die Dichtung, meine Damen und Herren—: diese Unendlichsprechung von lauter Sterblichkeit und Umsonst!"

24. Jacques Derrida, *Aporias*, trans. Thomas Dutoit (Stanford: Stanford University Press, 1993), 74. The word *shibboleth* shows up occasionally in texts by Derrida from the later 1980s onward,

though mostly in passing: see, e.g., *The Gift of Death* (1999), trans. David Wills (Chicago: University of Chicago Press, 2008), 82, 88.

25. Paul Celan, *Werke: Historisch-kritische Ausgabe*, ed. Holger Gehle et al. (Frankfurt am Main: Suhrkamp, 2004), 4.2:187.

## 8. *Shibboleth*: Salcedo

1. On museumgoers suffering minor injuries, see Sarah Lyell, "Caution: Art Afoot," *New York Times*, December 11, 2007; on the dark thrill of the abyss, see Richard Dumont, "Doris Salcedo: A Glimpse into the Abyss," *The Telegraph*, October 9, 2007.

2. James Cartwright, "The Man Who Tore the Tate in Two: Stuart Smith on Making Doris Salcedo's *Shibboleth* a Reality," *It's Nice That* (June 2, 2015; accessed June 5, 2019). Smith, a structural engineer hired by the Tate to help realize Salcedo's vision, laid down a slab into which the work, which Salcedo constructed in sections in her workshop in Colombia, was painstakingly set in such a way as to allow the fissure to appear "imperceptibly deep." Cartwright's informative article, centered on the figure of the male engineer who solves a tricky problem, exemplifies the kind of response that has reportedly caused Salcedo to feel that *Shibboleth* was not an unqualified success. See Mary Schneider Enriquez, *Doris Salcedo: The Materiality of Mourning* (Cambridge, MA: Harvard Art Museums, distributed by Yale University Press, 2017), 114 and 118n89, where Enriquez reports that in a discussion she held with Salcedo, the artist "gave *Shibboleth* as an example of a work that did not achieve what she sought to address to viewers."

3. For good discussions of this artwork, and of Salcedo's work generally, see Mieke Bal, *Of What One Cannot Speak: Doris Salcedo's Political Art* (Chicago: University of Chicago Press, 2010); Rebecca Comay, "Material Remains: Doris Salcedo," *The Oxford Literary Review* 39, no. 1 (2017): 42–64; Claudette Lauzon, *The Unmaking of Home in Contemporary Art* (Toronto: University of Toronto Press, 2017), esp. 137–139 and 174–175. All of these skilled readers grant only brief attention to the title "Shibboleth."

4. Salcedo's engagement with Celan's writing is long-standing and wide-ranging. The three *Unland* sculptures, *Unland: Irreversible Witness* (1995–98), *Unland: The Orphan's Tunic* (1997), and *Unland: Audible in the Mouth* (1998), draw their subtitles from lines from poems that appear in three different volumes of Celan's poetry: from (in the order given above) "Weggebeizt" ("Etched Away") in *Atemwende* (1967), "Ihn ritt die Nacht" ("Night Rode Him") in *Lichtzwang* (1970), and "Ein Auge, Offen" ("An Eye, Open") in *Sprachgitter* (1959). For her "Artist's Choice" selections in the collection *Doris Salcedo*, by Nancy Princenthal, Carlos Basualdo, and Andreas Huyssen (London: Phaidon Press, 2000), Salcedo chose lines from four relatively little-known Celan poems: in order, "Mit den Verfolgten" ("With the Persecuted") from *Atemwende*; "Ein Stern" ("A Star") an uncollected poem from 1969 (Paul Celan, *Die Gedichte, Neue kommentierte Gesamtausgabe in einem Band*, ed. Barbara Wiedemann ([Frankfurt am Main: Suhrkamp, 2018], 569); "Stehen im Schatten" ("To Stand in the Shadow") from *Atemwende*; "Kleine Nacht" ("Little Night") another uncollected poem from 1969 (564) (for the extracts, see *Doris Salcedo* 106, 108, 111, and 113). Salcedo's short foreword to Enriquez, *Doris Salcedo*, cites from *The Meridian* (and quotes lines from Mandelstam, and refers tellingly to Hannah Arendt, Giorgio Agamben, Jacques Derrida, Jacques Lacan, and other thinkers): see "From the Artist" in Enriquez, *Doris Salcedo*, xvii–xviii.

5. Adorno's emphasis on the irreducible element of protest in art is surely relevant for Salcedo's aesthetic: "All artworks, even the affirmative, are a priori polemical. . . . By emphatically separating themselves from the empirical world, they bear witness that the world itself should be other than it is." *Ästhetische Theorie, Gesammelte Schriften*, ed. Rolf Tiedemann et al. (Frankfurt am Main: Suhrkamp, 1977) 7: 264; *Aesthetic Theory*, trans. Robert Hullot-Kentor (Minneapolis: University of Minnesota Press, 1997),177.

6. Salcedo comments on *Shibboleth* in a video accessible through khanacademy.org (accessed June 29, 2019). She stresses that the work addresses racism and immigration, refers at one

point to Adorno, and hopes that visitors to the installation will "get the feeling of catastrophe in there" when they peer into the fissure.

7. This is a subject on which Derrida frequently wrote; see, as one text among many, "Title (to be specified)," trans. Tom Conley, *SubStance* 10, no. 2 (1981): 4–22.

8. J. L. Austin, *How To Do Things With Words*, 2nd ed., ed. J. O. Urmson and Marina Sbisà (Cambridge, MA: Harvard University Press, 1975), 22, italics in the original.

9. Paul Celan, *Werke: Historisch-kritische Ausgabe*, ed. Holger Gehle et al. (Frankfurt am Main: Suhrkamp, 2004), 4.2:187. "Call the shibboleth,/in it the dead meet each other."

# Index

Abraham (Biblical character), 30, 118n3
Abraham, Nicolas, 116n23
Adorno, Theodor W., 9, 89–90, 104, 114–115n20, 144n14, 147n10, 152n5, 152–153n6
Agamben, Giorgio, 152n4
Althusser, Louis, 23
Améry, Jean, 145n18
Ammonites, 7, 14–15
Apter, Emily, 5, 112n11, 112–113n13
Arendt, Hannah, 152n4
Aristotle, 149n21
Austin, J. L., 105–106; 153n8

Babel, 20, 34, 90–94, 96–97, 127n21, 148n14, 148–149n15. *See also* Bible: Genesis; Bruegel, Pieter, the elder; Derrida, Jacques: "Tours de Babel, Des"
Bachmann, Ingeborg, 146–147n4
Bail, Ulrike, 139–140n1
Bal, Mieke, 103, 118n1, 151n3
Balibar, Etienne, 121n2

Balzac, Honoré de, 110n4, 113–114n16
Basualdo, Carlos, 152n4
Bender, Hans. *See* Celan: "Letter to Hans Bender"
Benjamin, tribe of, 13–14, 18, 118n1
Benjamin, Walter, 1, 9, 63, 92, 109n1, 140n3, 149n17
Bergvall, Caroline, 120–121n1
Bible, 1, 14–15, 18, 88–91, 109–110n3, 119–120n8, 124–125n13, 125n16, 136–137n13, 149n20; Acts, 150n22; Acts 2, 94–95; 1 Corinthians, 96, 150n22; Deuteronomy, 22, 46, 118n3, 119–120n8; Exodus, 149n20; Ezekiel, 118n2; Genesis, 20, 90–91, 109n2, 119–120n8, 127n21; Isaiah, 1, 30, 109n2; Jeremiah, 118n2; Job, 1, 143n12; Joshua, 119–120n8; Judges, 2, 3, 7, 11, 13–18, 23, 26, 102, 109–110n3, 110n5, 113n15, 118nn1–2, 118–119n4, 119nn5,7, 121–122n6; 2 Kings, 118nn2–3; Leviticus, 118nn2–3;

155

Bible (cont.)
Luke, 77; Micah, 118n2; Numbers, 119–120n8, 143n12; Psalms, 1, 119–120n8, 143n12; Revelations, 66; Ruth, 109n2. *See also* Babel; Ephraim, tribe of; Gileadites; Jephthah
Blanchot, Maurice, 137n16
Blum, Leon, 132–133n3
Blum, Robert, 129n11
Boyer, Jean Pierre, 129–130n13
Bruegel, Pieter, the elder, 91–92, 148n14
Büchner, Georg, 38–39, 59–61, 63, 77, 79, 128n4, 136n12, 139nn21–22. *See also* Celan: *Meridian*
Buck, Theo, 139–140n1
Burke, Edmund, 55
Butler, Judith, 122n7
Byron, George Gordon, Lord, 113n15, 113–114n16

Cartwright, James, 151n2
Cavenagh, Clare, 135–136n11
Celan, Paul, 9, 11–12, 29, 36–42, 46–53, 55–56, 58–59, 61, 63–65, 68–70, 73–74, 76–79, 81, 83–90, 97–99, 102, 105–106, 117n27, 126n17, 127n3, 128n14–5, 129n8, 131n16, 131–132n17, 132n1, 132–133n3, 133n4, 133–134n7, 135n10, 135–136n11, 136–137n13, 137nn14,15, 138nn18,20, 139nn21–22, 139–140n1, 140n4, 141n7, 141–142n8, 142–143n9, 143nn10–11, 143–144n13, 144n14, 145n18, 146n22, 146n3, 146–147n4, 147n7, 148–149n15, 150n23, 151n25, 152n4, 153n9; "Ansprache anlässlich der Entgegennahme des Literaturpreises der Freien Hansestadt Bremen," 42, 79, 86–87, 146nn2–3; "Antwort auf eine Umfrage der Librairie Flinker," 48–49, 131–132n17; "Aschenglorie," 129n8; *Atemwende*, 97, 148–149n15, 152n4; "Auge, Offen, Ein," 152n4; "Conversation in the Mountains," 39; "Dein vom Wachen," 47; "Du liegst im großen Gelausche," 36; "Einem, der vor der Tür stand," 131n16; "Engführung," 74, 141n5; *Gedichte: Neue kommentierte Gesamtausgabe in einem Band*, 76, 78, 80, 89, 132n1, 133n4, 133–134n7, 136n12, 136–137n13, 139–140n1, 140n4, 141–142n8, 145n18, 147n7, 148–149n15, 152n4; "Gespräch im Gebirg," 39, 144n14; "Give the Word," 97–98; "Halbe Nacht," 144n15; "Hinausgekrönt," 71, 140n4, 148–149n15; "Ihn ritt die Nacht," 152n4; "In eins," 12, 40, 50–60, 62, 65, 69–71, 84–85, 133n4, 133–134n7, 135–136n11, 138nn19–20, 139–140nn1,4, 141–142n8, 148–149n15; "Kleine Nacht," 152n4; "Letter to Hans Bender," 137n15; *Lichtzwang*, 152n4; *Meridian*, 38–40, 61, 63–65, 68, 79–80, 98, 102, 117n27, 127–128n3, 128nn4–5, 133–134n7, 137nn14–15, 139n22, 143–144n13, 144n14, 150n23, 152n4; "Mit den Verfolgten," 152n4; *Mohn und Gedächtnis*, 144n15; *Niemandsrose, Die*, 50, 59, 71, 80, 148–149n15; "Poetry of Osip Mandelstam, The," 144n14; "Psalm," 148–149n15; "Radix, Matrix," 144n14, 145n18; "Rebleute graben," 144n14; "Schibboleth," 12, 50–52, 56, 69–85, 98–99, 102, 106, 132n1, 133–134n7, 139–140n1, 140n4, 141–142n8; *Sprachgitter*, 39,

141n5, 152n4; "Stehen im Schatten," 152n4; "Stern, Ein," 152n4; "Stimmen," 39–40, 137n15; "Todesfüge," 87, 146–147n4; "Todtnauberg," 138n18; "Unstetes Herz," 144n15; *Von Schwelle zu Schwelle*, 50, 69, 71, 133–134n7, 145n17; "Von Ungeträumtem," 148n15; "Weggebeizt," 152n4; *Werke: Historisch-Kritische Ausgabe*, 133n4,141–142n8, 151n25, 153n9; "Wurfholz, Ein," 144n14
Chalfen, Israel, 143n11, 146n1
Chiva, Isac, 78, 89, 132n1, 141–142n8
Coleridge, Hartley, 113n15
Coleridge, Samuel Taylor, 113n15
Comay, Rebecca, 103–104, 151n3
Culler, Jonathan, 80–81, 145n20, 145–146n21

Dante, 135–136n11
Dávidházi, Péter, 124–125n13
Deleuze, Gilles, 121n3
de Man, Paul, 81, 145–146n21
Derrida, Jacques, 11–12, 23–27, 31–32, 34–35, 37, 40–42, 46–47, 49–50, 53–54, 56, 59, 61–63, 65, 69–71, 84, 88, 92, 97–98, 102, 106, 116n23, 117nn26–27, 121–122n6, 123nn8,11, 125n15, 126nn18–19, 126–127n20, 127n21, 127n2, 127–128n3, 128n5, 128–129n7, 129nn8,10, 131nn15–16, 133nn5–6, 133–134n7, 137n14, 140n2, 143–144n13, 147n6, 149n16, 150n23, 150–151n24, 152n4, 153n7; "Afterword: Toward an Ethic of Discussion," 27–28, 123n11; *Aporias*, 98, 150–151n24; "Autoimmunity: Real and Symbolic Suicides," 128–129n7; *Beast and the Sovereign*, 128n5; "Fors," 116n23; *Gift of Death, The*, 150–151n24; *Limited Inc*, 28, 117n26, 123n11; "Limited Inc a b c . . . ," 117n26; "Majesties," 128n5; *Memoires for Paul de Man*, 34, 126n19; *Monolingualism of the Other*, 34, 88, 126n18, 147n6; *Of Grammatology*, 42, 129n10; *On Touching—Jean-Luc Nancy*, 131n15; *Rogues: Two Essays on Reason*, 31–32, 125n15; *Schibboleth: Pour Paul Celan*, 11, 117n27, 126n19; *Shibboleth: For Paul Celan*, 12, 23, 25–26, 30–31, 34–35, 37, 40–42, 46–49, 53, 59, 62, 65, 69–70, 97, 102, 117n27, 121–122n6, 127n2, 128n5, 133n6, 140n2, 149n16; "Signature Event Context," 117n26; *Sovereignties in Question: The Poetics of Paul Celan*, 117n27, 121–122n6, 127nn2–3, 128n5, 133n6, 133–134n7, 140n2, 143–144n13, 149n16, 150n23; *Specters of Marx: The State of Debt, the Work of Mourning, and the New International*, 126–127n20; "Title (to be specified)," 153n7; "Tours de Babel, Des," 35, 127n21; "White Mythology: Metaphor in the Text of Philosophy," 25, 123n8
de Vries, Hent, 41, 129n9
Dmitrieva-Einhorn, Marina, 143n11
Dollfuss, Engelbert, 52, 132n2
Dryden, John, 113n15
Dumont, Richard, 151n1

Einhorn, Erich, 143n11
Eluard, Paul, 71, 140n4
Enriquez, Mary Schneider, 151n2, 152n4

Ephraim, tribe of, 2–3, 7, 11, 14–18, 20–23, 28–30, 33, 84, 110n4, 111n6, 111–112n8, 118–119n4, 119–120n8, 121–122n6, 125–126n16. *See also* Bible: Judges; Gileadites; Jephthah

Facebook, 5
Faulkner, William, 8, 42, 44, 114n17, 123n10, 129n12, 129–130n13; *Absalom, Absalom!*, 8–9, 25, 42–45, 114n17, 123n10, 129n12, 129–130n13, 130–131n14, 131n15
Fichte, Johann Gottlieb, 9, 21, 121n2
Flinker, Martin, 131–32n17. *See also* Celan: "Antwort auf eine Umfrage der Librairie Flinker"
Franco, Francisco, 53, 142–143n9, 144–145n16
Franzos, Karl Emil, 128n4
Freud, Sigmund, 9–10, 116n23
Fynsk, Christopher, 64, 137–138n17, 146n3

Gadamer, Hans-Georg, 144n14
Gibson, William, 93, 149n18
Gideon (Biblical character), 7, 18, 113n15
Gileadites, 2–3, 7, 14–18, 20–22, 28–30, 33, 84, 111n6, 111–112n8, 118–119n4, 119–120n8. *See also* Bible: Judges; Ephraim, tribe of; Jephthah
Glazova, Anna, 135–136n11
Gobineau, Arthur de, 29, 123–124n12
Goethe, J. W., 114n19; *Faust*, 134n9
Goll affair, 131–132n17, 141–142n8
Goll, Claire, 132n17
Goll, Yvan, 132n17
Gómez, Dolores Ibárruri, 53
Google, 93
Gosling, F. A., 119–120n8
Govain, Renaud, 120–121n1

Haitian revolution, 42–45, 129–130n13
Hamlin, E. John, 118n2
Hegel, G. W. F., 9, 50, 114–115nn20–21
Heidegger, Martin, 64, 137–138n17, 138n18, 146n3
Hiebert, Theodore, 91, 148n13
Hinderer, Walter, 128n4
Hitler, Adolph, 129n11
Holocaust, the, 36, 39, 89
Huyssen, Andreas, 152n4

Jacob (Biblical character), 119–120n8
Janz, Marlies, 132–133n3, 135–136n11, 139–140n1
Jephthah (Biblical character), 3, 7, 14–15, 17–18, 27, 29, 32, 110n5, 111n6, 113n15, 118nn2–3, 119nn6–7, 119–120n8, 124–125n13, 125–126n16. *See also* Bible: Judges; Ephraim, tribe of; Gileadites
Jerome. *See* St. Jerome
Johnson, Samuel, 111–112n8
Joyce, James, 33, 126n17
Judges. *See* Bible: Judges

Kafka, Franz, 114n19
Kant, Immanuel, 9
Keats, John, 81
Khalip, Jacques, 129n8
Kirchhoff, Gerhard, 76, 78
Koehler, Ludwig, 109n2
Koerner, Joseph Leo, 148n14
Kraus, Karl, 1, 109n1

Lacan, Jacques, 23, 30, 122n7, 125n14, 152n4
Lacoue-Labarthe, Philippe, 40, 123–124n12, 128n6

# INDEX

Larsen, Nella, 123n10
Lauzon, Claudette, 104, 151n3
Lenin, Vladimir, 134n8
Levinas, Emmanuel, 102
Levine, Michael G., 47, 63, 128n4, 131n16, 132–133n3, 139–140n1, 146n3
Liebknecht, Karl, 37
Lingis, Alphonso, 5, 112n10
Lukács, Georg, 134n8
Luther, Martin, 76, 143n12
Luxemburg, Rosa, 37, 134n8
Lyell, Sarah, 151n1

Maher, Ciarán, 120–121n1
Manasseh, tribe of, 16, 18, 119–120n8
Mandelstam, Osip, 59, 67, 74, 135–136n11, 138n20, 141n7, 144n14, 148–149n15, 152n4. *See also* Celan: "In eins," "Poetry of Osip Mandelstam, The"
Marks, Hebert, 149n20
Marvell, Andrew, 113n15, 113–114n16
Marx, Karl, 9, 50, 114–115nn20–21, 134n8
Matins of Bruges, 19–20, 120–121n1
Matthews, John T., 44, 129–130n13
Mendicino, Kristina, 68, 139n22
Midianites, 7, 18, 113n15
Mieszkowski, Jan, 134n8
Milton, John, 7–8, 113n15
Moabites, 18
Moses (Biblical character), 46, 119–120n8, 143n12, 149n20
Müller-Sievers, Helmut, 139n22

Nail, Thomas, 121n3
Nancy, Jean-Luc, 62, 123–124n12, 137n16
Neumann, Peter Horst, 139–140n1
Nietzsche, Friedrich, 9

Oberlin, Johann Friedrich, 128n4
Ophir, Adi, 125–126n16
Ovid, 135–36n11; *Metamorphoses*, 74

Quintilian, 80, 82, 145n19

Parsley Massacre, 20, 120–121n1
Paul. *See* St. Paul
Peter. *See* St. Peter
Petrarch, 66
Poe, Edgar Allan, 11, 101, 116–117n24
Pöggeler, Otto, 138n18
Princenthal, Nancy, 152n4

Rabelais, François, 113–114n16
Redfield, Marc, 122n7, 128–129n7, 129n11
Rendsburg, Gary A., 118–119n4
Reuben, tribe of, 119–120n8
Richard, Arnaud, 120–121n1
Richter, Gerhard, 113–114n16, 114–115n20
Ronell, Avital, 113n14
Rousseau, Jean-Jacques, 25, 28, 123n9
Russian revolution, 52, 59–60, 138n19

Salcedo, Doris, 12, 100–102, 104–106, 151nn2–3, 152nn4–5, 152–153n6; *Shibboleth*, 12, 100–103, 105–106, 151n2, 152n4, 152–153n6; *Unland*, 102, 105, 152n4
Samson (Biblical character), 7–8, 113n15
Sasson, Jack M., 16–17, 119nn5–7
Saussure, Ferdinand de, 23, 68, 121n5
Schestag, Thomas, 87, 134n9, 145n18, 147n5
Schiller, Friedrich, 114n19
Schmitt, Carl, 22, 26, 29, 31, 90, 121n4, 148n12

Schneider, Tammi, 118n2, 125–126n16
Schuschnigg, Kurt, 132n2
Scott, Walter, 113–114n16
Septuagint, 96–97, 109–110n3
Shakespeare, William, 124–125n13; *Hamlet*, 34, 124–125n13, 126–127n20; *King Lear*, 98
Shepherdson, Charles, 122n7
Sicilian Vespers, 19
Smelik, Willem F., 119n7, 121–122n6
Smith, Stuart, 151n2
Spanish Civil War, 52–55, 60, 77–78, 139–140n1, 142–143n9, 144–145n16
Speiser, E. A., 118–119n4
Spurr, Thomas, 139–140n1
St. Jerome, 109–110n3
St. Paul, 46, 96, 150n22
St. Peter, 95
Swiggers, P., 118–119n4
Szondi, Peter, 36–37, 74, 127n1, 141n5

Todd, H. J., 111–112n8
Torok, Maria, 116n23
Tower of Babel, the. *See* Babel

Trujillo, Rafael, 20. *See also* Parsley Massacre

Voltaire, 127n21

Wachsmann, Nikolaus, 141n6
Wagner, Richard, 123–124n12
Waldrop, Rosemarie, 131–132n17
Weber, Samuel, 117n26, 140n3, 149n17
Weidig, Friedrich Ludwig, 136n12, 139n21
Weizman, Eyal, 112–113n13
Wiedemann, Barbara, 133n4, 136n12, 136–137n13, 140n4, 141–142n8, 143n11, 145n18, 147n7. *See also* Celan: *Gedichte: Neue kommentierte Gesamtausgabe in einem Band*
Wolskij, Alexi, 141n7
Wordsworth, William, 49

Yagüe, Juan, 144–145n16
Yildiz, Yasemin, 147n8
Yiphtah. *See* Jephthah

Zweig, Stefan, 135–136n11

MARC REDFIELD is Chair of the Department of Comparative Literature and Professor of Comparative Literature, English, and German at Brown University. His most recent books are *The Rhetoric of Terror: Reflections on 9/11 and the War on Terror* (Fordham University Press, 2009) and *Theory at Yale: The Strange Case of Deconstruction in America* (Fordham University Press, 2016).

Sara Guyer and Brian McGrath, series editors

Sara Guyer, *Reading with John Clare: Biopoetics, Sovereignty, Romanticism.*

Philippe Lacoue-Labarthe, *Ending and Unending Agony: On Maurice Blanchot.* Translated by Hannes Opelz.

Emily Rohrbach, *Modernity's Mist: British Romanticism and the Poetics of Anticipation.*

Marc Redfield, *Theory at Yale: The Strange Case of Deconstruction in America.*

Jacques Khalip and Forest Pyle (Eds.), *Constellations of a Contemporary Romanticism.*

Geoffrey Bennington, *Kant on the Frontier: Philosophy, Politics, and the Ends of the Earth.*

Frédéric Neyrat, *Atopias: Manifesto for a Radical Existentialism.* Translated by Walt Hunter and Lindsay Turner, Foreword by Steven Shaviro.

Jacques Khalip, *Last Things: Disastrous Form from Kant to Hujar.*

Jacques Lezra, *On the Nature of Marx's Things: Translation as Necrophilology.* Foreword by Vittorio Morfino.

Jean-Luc Nancy, *Portrait*. Translated by Sarah Clift and Simon Sparks, Foreword by Jeffrey S. Librett.

Karen Swann, *Lives of the Dead Poets: Keats, Shelley, Coleridge*.

Erin Graff Zivin, *Anarchaelogies: Reading as Misreading*.

Ramsey McGlazer, *Old Schools: Modernism, Education, and the Critique of Progress*.

Zachary Sng, *Middling Romanticism: Reading in the Gaps, from Kant to Ashbery*.

www.ingramcontent.com/pod-product-compliance
Lightning Source LLC
Chambersburg PA
CBHW020110020526
44112CB00033B/1139